Be What God Has Made You
Living Your Identity In Christ

Be What God Has Made You

Living Your Identity In Christ

By Chris J. Pluger

Distributed by CreateSpace

© 2012, Chris J. Pluger

ISBN-13: 978-1479266722
ISBN-10: 1479266728

Scripture quotations, unless otherwise noted, are taken from the HOLY BIBLE, NEW INTERNATIONAL VERSION® (NIV). Copyright © 1973, 1978, 1984 International Bible Society. Used by permission of Zondervan. All rights reserved.

Cover photos by Jordan E. Cave

Printed in the United States of America

Dedication

To the faculty, staff, and students of the Christian schools of which I have been a part:

NWC
MLC
WLS
WLHS
ECA
BLS
GIAL

Author's Note

I wrote these devotions originally for the staff at a Christian school where I taught for three years. I wrote one each week for a year, following an outline I worked up over the summer. At the end, I felt like I had a nice collection.

Now, years later, I've taken them out, dusted them off, edited them slightly for a wider audience, and present them to you with the prayer that something I wrote will help you in your journey to be more like Jesus.

Nothing in this book is original to me. The title encouragement to "Be what God has made you" comes from a college professor. Many of the "identities" I have discussed came from a poster I saw once and thought to copy down. Several of the devotions owe a lot to images and words from J. A. O. Preus' *Just Words: Understanding the Fullness of the Gospel*, which is a much better book than this one is. There are quotations all over the book by people who express an idea far better than I ever could. And I pray that the theology is Biblical, and certainly not original to me.

Nevertheless, I am confident that the reader will find something of value, which will make it worth my time to (re)publish these devotions. At the very least, God has made me a writer – and in being what God has made me, I *must* write.

Chris Pluger
Zambia
September 2012

Table of Contents

I. In your relationship with *Himself*, God has made you…

    His child 21
    Alive with Christ 25
    Free from condemnation 29
    Righteous 33
    Redeemed 37
    Reconciled 41
    At peace 45
    A "free slave" 49
    A "living sacrifice" 53

II. In your relationship with *yourself*, God has made you…

    A new creation 59
    Confident in the faith 63
    An imitator of God 67
    Able to do everything 71
    Strong in his mighty power 75
    A jar of clay 79
    Dead to sin 83

III. In your relationships with *other believers*, God has made you…

    A living stone in a spiritual house 89
    A part of the Body of Christ 93
    A branch of the True Vine 97
    A royal priest 101
    Devoted to prayer 105
    A minister of reconciliation 109
    Your brother's keeper 113

IV. In your relationship to *the world*, God has made you…

An alien and a stranger 119
Salt and light 123
Hated 127
An enemy of the prince of the world 131
His ambassador 135
Rescued from the dominion of darkness 139
More than a conqueror 143
Conclusion...147

Introduction:
Be What God Has Made You!

Only let us live up to what we have already attained. (Philippians 3:16)

It is one of the great truths of Christianity that the Lord never tells us to do something that he doesn't also give us the ability to do. When Christ gave the Apostles the Great Commission — the command to spread the Gospel — he also gave them the ability to carry it out. He sent them out into a world that he had specifically prepared for the massive amount of evangelism that would be done. The apostles had the advantages of a universal language, widespread peace, relatively convenient travel, a core group of Jewish believers in every major metropolis who knew the Old Testament and its promises, and a culture of people who were growing disinterested in the old Roman gods and longing to fill the spiritual void in their lives.

Today, the Great Commission is still being fulfilled by believers who have access to air travel, instantaneous global telecommunication, a Bible that has been translated into thousands of languages, and an abundance of Bible-study resources. In addition to those external advantages,

God the Holy Spirit works in the hearts of all believers, ancient and modern, to create and sustain faith in Jesus as God's Son, the Savior.

Evangelism is but one example of this great Truth. No matter what the command, the Lord always gives his people the ability to do what he has told them. God does not push us out of the nest, so to speak, to learn to fly on our own. Contrary to the popular expression, God does not help those who help themselves — in fact, theologically speaking, none of us can help ourselves, nor do we even want to. We were steeped in rebellion and sin at birth, and we stubbornly stay that way until God himself acts on our stony sinful hearts. Paul writes in Philippians 2:13, "It is God who works in you to *will* and to *act* according to his good purpose." Not only the *doing*, but even the *wanting to do* is the work of the Lord. We do not count on ourselves for the ability to carry our God's commands. Instead, we count on God.

It is this great Biblical truth that inspires the theme for this small book: *Be what God has made you!* The words are simple. The message is clear. God has never told us to do something he has not given us the ability to do. God has not told us to be anything he hasn't already made us in Christ Jesus, either. The Bible is full of descriptions of believers' new identity in Christ: we are his children, new creations, dead to sin, the Body of Christ, aliens and strangers, salt and light — the list goes on and on. When God gives us a command, he gives us the power to do it. When God says "believe," he also sends his Holy Spirit to create faith in our hearts. When he tells us to "be," he also makes us into what he wants is to be.

We are not being asked to pull ourselves up by our own bootstraps, to do a better (or perfect) job with our own energy and strength. Such a human effort would be impossible! No, we are told simply to be what God has already made us. We are encouraged (and we encourage others) to live up to who we are in Christ — not so that we become holy, but because we already are. Philippians 3:16 says, "Let us live up to what we have already attained." *Already attained* — it is God who has done all the work; it is God who receives all the glory.

See the distinction between the commands of God and his promises? By our own power, we cannot do what God tells us to do. And because we cannot fulfill the Law's commands, we deserve eternal condemnation in hell. Everything we do without faith in Christ is driving us ruthlessly down the wide, long road to eternal separation from God in hell. Without God to make us new people, we are lost.

But thanks be to God! He has rescued us from ourselves, and sent Christ to fulfill our obligation to the Law and to pay our debt in full. There is no condemnation for those who are in Christ Jesus (Romans 8:1)! If anyone is in Christ, he is a new creation — the old has gone, the new has come (2 Corinthians 5:17)! The pure message of the Gospel promises us that God, in Christ, has made us holy, forgiven, children and heirs of eternal life. In Christ, he has once again given us the ability to carry out what he asks us to do.

And now, Christian: Be what God has made you! Be what you are, without regard for the foolishness of your flesh or the denials of the devil or the wiles of the world. No excuses. Don't spend another minute living in the sin that takes you away from God. You died to sin — how can you live in it any longer? God has made you holy. Be holy!

This book is divided into four sections, each looking at the identity we have in Christ — what God has made us — in a different set of relationships. The first is our relationship to God: how has he changed our identity, and our relationship with himself along the way? The second relationship is our relationship to ourselves: what new self-identity do I have because of Jesus' work? The last two deal with our relationships to others, first to other believers and then to the world at large: how does my new identity in Christ, and my new standing with God, affect my relationship with my neighbors and the world?

Throughout this book, we will look deeply into the face of Christ, who gave his life for us and whose identity is now ours through faith. As we read, we will be strengthened in faith and guided in holiness as we look to God's Word and consider how best to be what God has made us — how best to "live up to what we have already attained."

We have been given a new standing before God, and have been saved — now and for eternity — by Jesus' incarnation, his perfect life, innocent death and glorious resurrection. We are sanctified, able to live new and holy lives by the power of the

Holy Spirit who comes to us by, through, and in the Word and Sacraments. We act like who we are. "Let us live up to what we have already attained."

May God be with us and have mercy on us for Jesus' sake.

Part One:
Your Relationship to God

Be What God Has Made You: His Child!

Those who are led by the Spirit of God are sons of God. For you did not receive a spirit that makes you a slave again to fear, but you received the Spirit of sonship. And by him we cry, "Abba, Father." The Spirit himself testifies with our spirit that we are God's children. (Romans 8:14-16)

A question to ponder: why do we like babies so much?

Evolutionary biologists say that we like babies because their cuteness is a natural survival mechanism, developed over millions of years to make sure that babies make it to adulthood. We look into those adorable little eyes and just want to feed them, clothe them, and take care of them.

Maybe we like babies because of all of the positive feedback we get from them. Think of it as a you-scratch-my-back-and-I'll-scratch-yours kind of thing — hours of feeding and diapering and cleaning and seemingly endless tasks of parenting for what? A little coo and a smile?

OK, that's a little harsh. We must like our babies because we can imagine what they will become. I look at my son and wonder with amazement at what he will become in 5, 10, 20, or

30 years. I can think of all the things God has planned for him, how my wonderful parenting will obviously produce a wonderful child who will do wonderful things for those around him. I can think of how he will grow up to save money, or save lives, or save souls, or save me.

Those explanations don't really answer the question, though, do they? Ugly babies are still loved by their parents. Needy babies are still loved by their parents. And kids who don't live up to Daddy's expectations are still loved just as nearly and dearly.

So... dare I venture to say it? I think that we love babies not because of something in them, but because of something in us. Even though we are imperfect and make mistakes and love selfishly, Jesus said that even we know how to give good gifts to our children—and the greatest of these is love. As parents we love our kids with a love that is a pale reflection of the perfect unselfish *agape* love that the Father first lavished on us.

If we love our children not because of something that they give to us, but because of something in our own nature as parents, then how much more is God's love for us based not on something in us, but on something in God's own nature that causes him to love us? After all, "God is love" (1 John 4:16).

"How great is the love the Father has lavished on us, that we should be called children of God!" (1 John 3:1). How great indeed! He lavished his love upon us in Christ "while we were still sinners" (Romans 5:8). It wasn't because we were lovable, or cute, or good, or so full of spiritual religious potential that God loved us and called us his children, but "because of his great love for us" (Ephesians 2:4).

You are a child of God, the heavenly Father. You have been "adopted" by God (Ephesians 1:4-6). You are a part of God's family, one of his own, dear children. To use Paul's legal, Roman, metaphor, we have "the full rights of sons" (Galatians 4:5). We are "co-heirs with Christ" — we, as God's adopted sons and daughters, will have a part in everything that Jesus has. "We share in his sufferings in order that we may also share in his glory" (Romans 8:17).

You are a child of God, the heavenly Father. The book of Hebrews reminds us of another thing we can expect as children of God: discipline. When God sends us trials, he is treating us as his children. "Endure hardship as discipline; God is treating you as sons... Our fathers disciplined us for a little while as they thought best; but God disciplines us for our good, that we may share in his holiness" (Hebrews 12:7-10). Our Father loves us and cares for us, and one way he shows that love is by disciplining us so that we grow into ever more fruitful and productive children.

You are a child of God, the heavenly Father. You are loved with a love that does not depend on your "loveableness," but on God's divine and unchanging grace. You are loved with a love that does not wax and wane with your unfaithfulness, but flows from the heart of God, who demonstrated his love for us on Calvary's cross. You have the full rights of a child of God. Your spirit can cry "Abba, Father!" with the boldness and confidence that he hears your prayer. You are disciplined as a child, so that you may someday share in Christ's holiness.

You are a child of God, the heavenly Father. Be what God has made you!

✠

Be What God Has Made You: Alive With Christ!

When you were dead in your sins and in the uncircumcision of your sinful nature, God made you alive with Christ. He forgave us all our sins, having canceled the written code, with its regulations, that was against us and that stood opposed to us; he took it away, nailing it to the cross. And having disarmed the powers and authorities, he made a public spectacle of them, triumphing over them by the cross. (Colossians 2:13-15)

A lone figure walks through cold, windswept city streets in the quickly-fading light of a dark and rainy evening. Wind whips the figure's black coat and sweeps away the hollow echoes of hurried footfalls on concrete. Mounting a set of stairs two at a time, the figure strides in through the glass doors of a nondescript government building. He stops at the guards' desk, signs a form on a clipboard, and receives a visitor's pass. More footfalls, more doors, more clipboards, and the figure finds himself in a long, narrow room, freezing cold and erratically lit by stuttering fluorescent lights: the city morgue.

A white-coated technician leads him past row upon row of stainless steel doors, set three high in the green-tiled wall. They stop in front of the one indicated by a number on yet another clipboard. At a nod from the first man, the technician opens the door and slides out the table. A cloth-enshrouded body lies rigid on the tray. Another nod. The sheet is pulled back to reveal the corpse's face.

It's you. Your own face. Your body lies cold and unmoving on that anonymous, dehumanizing steel. The dark-suited figure shakes his head, once, half in pity. The drawer slides back. The door closes, locking you in. *Click.* You are dead.

Dead. What a horrible word. Dead is beyond life, beyond hope; powerless, empty, futile, lost. And as terrifying as death is, as far from the warm safe happy glow of life that we now enjoy, there was a time when each one of us was dead. Not dead physically, but dead spiritually. We were "dead in our transgressions and sins... gratifying the cravings of our sinful nature and following its desires and thoughts... by nature objects of wrath" (Ephesians 2:1-3).

By nature we were objects of God's wrath — dead in our sins and our sinful nature. Call it "Original Sin" and trace it all the way back to Adam (Romans 5:12). Or call it "total depravity" and remember that there is nothing at all good in any of us (Romans 7:18). Or simply recognize the full impact of the truth that you were once "dead in your sins." Whatever terminology you use, the truth is inescapable: without Christ, you are a dead body in a morgue, waiting until Judgment Day for God to cast you into hell forever. And there's nothing you can do about it.

A spiritually dead person can no more turn to Christ and be saved than a dead body can choose to come alive again. A dead body is powerless, without hope or ability or any motivation to help itself. It's just dead. A spiritually dead person is in a similarly un-fixable predicament. Sin is not only an insult to God and a transgression of his holy will, it is spiritual suicide — a willful destruction of God's image in us and a humanly-irreversible act of spiritual vandalism. To put it simply, sin kills.

But thanks be to God! What was impossible for man is possible with God (Mark 10:27). Completely on his own, without any help or cooperation or decision on our part — while we were dead — God made us "alive with Christ." He forgave all of our sins, which were like a self-inflicted stake in our hearts, and replaced our dead hearts of stone with living hearts of flesh (Ezekiel 36:26).

Death, our final enemy (1 Corinthians 15:26), has been vanquished. The "written code" of God's law, which stood condemning us, has been cancelled because it was fulfilled by Jesus (Matthew 5:17). Death and sin have no power over us; we are alive with Christ!

Christians of the Eastern Orthodox tradition sing a short hymn, or *troparion*, during the Easter season to celebrate Christ's victory over death on our behalf and the new life he gives us. "Christ is risen from the dead, trampling down death by death, and upon those in the tombs bestowing life."

We were in the tomb, spiritually dead in our sins since the time of our conception (Psalm 51:5). Someday, we will be in the tomb, physically dead because of the havoc that sin has wrought on the world (Romans 8:20-21). But Jesus has triumphed over the powers of sin and death by the cross. His victory is our victory.

"Christ Jesus has destroyed death and has brought life and immortality to light through the gospel" (2 Timothy 1:10). We are truly alive with Christ!

Be What God Has Made You: Free From Condemnation!

Therefore, there is now no condemnation for those who are in Christ Jesus, because through Christ Jesus the law of the Spirit of life set me free from the law of sin and death. For what the law was powerless to do in that it was weakened by the sinful nature, God did by sending his own Son in the likeness of sinful man to be a sin offering. And so he condemned sin in sinful man, in order that the righteous requirements of the law might be fully met in us, who do not live according to the sinful nature but according to the Spirit. (Romans 8:1-4)

The atmosphere in the courtroom is tense. Everyone stands. The judge enters. The defendant nervously fidgets. Eyes dart around the room. Breath is held. The verdict is read. "Not guilty!" Everything changes. Like a bursting dam, excitement spills out, replacing fear and anxiety. "You are free to go." Smiles. Handshakes. Freedom.

We, too, are declared "not guilty!" in God's courtroom. Although formerly we were under the judgment of God's Law (Romans 2:12), we are now "set free from law of sin and death" (8:2). The Law no longer holds us or condemns us. We are free to go, and to live our lives free from condemnation.

God's Law is powerful. It contains God's holy will and his righteous threats of condemnation for all those who violate it by unholy living. Ultimately, however, the Law is "powerless," because it is unable to *make* people holy. It can only tell us what to do, not give us the ability to do it. Paul says the Law is powerless, because people are powerless to obey it perfectly and the Law is powerless to help us. The best the Law can do is show us God's will, and then condemn us for not following it. The Law exposes our guilt because of sin, but does nothing to free us from it.

Martin Luther explains this way: "We must first of all learn from the perfectly clear Law our inability to obey it truly and according to God's will. Then we shall see that Christ is absolutely necessary as the giver of the Holy Spirit and of grace."

Christ is absolutely necessary, and his good news is this: what the Law was powerless to do — what we were powerless to do — God did (8:3). Remember, God never tells us to do anything he does not also do for us in Christ. Put it this way: in his Law, God tells us to "be perfect" (Matthew 5:48). But that command does not give us the power to be perfect. All that command can do is show us how far we fall from God's standards. All that command does is reveal how much we deserve God's righteous condemnation. But in the Gospel, the Good News, we see that that command is fulfilled in the life and death of Jesus Christ. What God has demanded — what we were powerless to do — God accomplished for us in Christ. We do not have to free ourselves. It is God who sets us free from the condemnation of the Law, sin, and death.

How does God set us free from this terrible condemnation? By ignoring our sin, and hoping it goes away? No. God is a righteous judge, who demands that sin be condemned and the requirements of the law be met. God set us free "by sending his own Son in the likeness of sinful man to be a sin offering" (8:3).

See again in this verse the idea of exchange: our sin for Christ's righteousness, our guilt for Christ's innocence. Everything that Christ has is ours by faith. The Innocent One is condemned so that the guilty go free.

"Christ Jesus... has become for us wisdom from God — that is, our righteousness, holiness and redemption" (1 Corinthians 1:30).

The holiness we have is not ours, but Christ's. God imputed it to us — put it on us — through faith. Theologians call this the idea of *Christus pro nobis* — Christ *for us*; that is, Christ in our place, Christ on our behalf, Christ in exchange for us.

When Jesus died on the cross, God condemned sin by condemning his Son, the sin-bearer. Sin no longer has the power to control us. It has no power to indict us. The righteous requirements of the law are "fully met in us," (8:4) because of Jesus' life and death *pro nobis*. We who are "in Christ Jesus" by faith are declared "not guilty" of sin.

We are free from condemnation. We no longer live as guilty sinners, looking over our shoulders in fear of the coming wrath. We have no reason to lie awake at night, terrified of our sins and the punishment that is due because of them. We do not need to fear God's righteous judgment on the Last Day, for "there is now no condemnation for those who are in Christ Jesus" (8:1).

We are in Christ Jesus, through faith in the promises of the Gospel. By the power of the Holy Spirit, we live as free people — not with licenses to sin (Jude 1:4; Galatians 5:13), but with joy, and "according to the Spirit" (8:4).

We were under the law of sin, condemned to death by the righteous requirements of the law. Now, through Christ, everything changes. We are declared "not guilty," set free from condemnation to live new, free lives according to the Spirit. Let us be what God has made us!

Be What God Has Made You: Righteous!

In the LORD *alone are righteousness and strength. All who have raged against him will come to him and be put to shame. But in the* LORD *all the descendants of Israel will be found righteous and will exult.* (Isaiah 45:24-25)

The word "righteous" is a common word in Scripture. It appears all over the Bible applied to many different things: God, believers, nations, laws, even pagan kings. But for all of the times we've read it, how well do we understand it? What does it mean to be "righteous"?

The most basic definition of "to be righteous" is "to conform to a standard." It's easy to see how God is righteous. In his sovereignty, God is completely above all human standards. Psalm 145:17 states, "The Lord is righteous in all his ways and holy in all his works." He is totally independent of any restrictions. He *is* the standard; he is the law. Deuteronomy 32:4 says, "He is the Rock, his works are perfect, and all his ways are just." God's essence sets the definition of righteousness for the rest of creation.

Human righteousness, then, is a reflection of God's perfect righteousness. A person exhibits righteousness by conforming to God's standards. It's not enough to do what is right in the eyes of our society, or our friends, or ourselves. Our bar is set much higher. We must conform to God himself.

There is only one problem with this standard of righteousness: it's impossible to achieve. There is no way that you or I, fallible creatures that we are, can ever for a second begin to measure up to God's righteousness. Humans cannot even touch the foot of the mountain of God's law (Exodus 19:12), much less attain to the heights of it.

Righteousness is conformity to a standard, and the standard which God sets is perfection. "Be holy because I, the LORD your God, am holy" (Leviticus 19:2). We fall far short of that standard every day. We make feeble attempts at righteousness, but in the end our works become twisted and poisoned evidence of our own self-righteousness. "All of us have become like one who is unclean, and all our righteous acts are like filthy rags." (Isaiah 64:6). So much for the "do it yourself" approach — if even our righteous acts are filthy; imagine our sins!

But Isaiah writes, "In the LORD alone are righteousness and strength... In the LORD all the descendants of Israel will be found righteous and will exult." Our righteousness is not something in us. It comes "in the LORD." In Psalm 72, Solomon prays, "Endow the king with your justice, O God, the royal son with your righteousness." Solomon knew that he needed the Lord's righteousness, because he had none of his own to offer.

Righteousness is a work of the Holy Spirit. The prophet Isaiah looked forward to the day when "the Spirit is poured upon us from on high, and… righteousness lives in the fertile field" (Isaiah 32:15,17). The Lord told Ezekiel, "I will put my Spirit in you, and move you to follow my decrees and be careful to keep my laws" (Ezekiel 36:27). Notice that it is the Lord himself who moves us to follow his decrees — our righteous conformity to God's holy standards is the work of God alone.

This righteousness comes to us by faith in God's promise of salvation, as Habakkuk writes, "The righteous will live by his faith." Abram, the father of believers, also received righteousness from God through faith: "Abram believed the LORD, and he credited it to him as righteousness" (Genesis 15:6). Six hundred years before the first Christmas, God promised through Jeremiah, "In those days and at that time I will make a righteous Branch sprout from David's line; he will do what is just and right in the land. In those days Judah will be saved and Jerusalem will live in safety. This is the name by which it will be called: The LORD Our Righteousness" (Jeremiah 33:15-17).

The Lord is our Righteousness. Jesus Christ, the God-Man, our Lord and Savior, is righteous and holy. He perfectly conformed to God's standard of perfection, and then perfectly submitted to God's will and died as our Substitute. God gives us his righteousness by faith in Christ, who is "The LORD Our Righteousness."

So, now what? Do we just sit around until Judgment Day "being righteous" without really doing anything? Of course not. For the time the Lord gives us, we follow the example of Noah, and Job, and Daniel, and countless other righteous people of faith. Out of love and thanksgiving, we obey God's Word. We strive to meet his standards. We live our lives according to his will, not because we have to be righteous, but because we are righteous. Let us be what God has made us!

Be What God Has Made You: Redeemed!

Christ redeemed us from the curse of the law by becoming a curse for us, for it is written: "Cursed is everyone who is hung on a tree." He redeemed us in order that the blessing given to Abraham might come to the Gentiles through Christ Jesus, so that by faith we might receive the promise of the Spirit. (Galatians 3:13-14)

The sun is blinding as you are dragged from the blackness of the wagon into the brilliant white light of day. You are shoved into a line with a dozen other captives, and the crack of a whip urges you forward. Your chalk-painted feet stumble on the way up the stairs to a rough-hewn wooden platform. The babble of voices in a strange tongue surrounds you, and the clinking of coins gives you an ominous premonition of what is about to happen. Rough hands prod and squeeze your skin. Your mouth is forced open for inspection. The chains around your wrists, which are the only thing you are wearing, are secured to a stout wooden post. Disinterested eyes coolly appraise your appearance, measuring your worth in two seconds' glance. The bidding commences…

Although the force of the word is mostly lost on us today, the word "redeem" transported a first-century Christian into the bustling arena of the slave market. The word "redeem" means to "buy back" or "purchase deliverance for." In the commercial language of the slave trade, a slave could often buy back his freedom, or "redeem himself" by earning enough money to pay his debt to his master.

In Galatians 3:2, Paul asks the people, "Did you receive the Spirit by observing the law, or by believing what you heard?" The obvious answer was "believing," and yet the Galatians had been led into error by people who said that while faith in Christ was important, "works of law" had to be added to secure salvation.

Paul then goes on to argue that salvation does not come through the law. He gives the example of Abraham, who was declared righteous not because he observed the law but "by faith" (v. 8). Then in verse 10, Paul writes, "All who rely on observing the law are under a curse, for it is written: 'Cursed is everyone who does not continue to do everything written in the Book of the Law.'" The law might have been enough to save us, had we been able to keep it perfectly, but because we don't fulfill it all, we are under God's curse. The law cannot save, only condemn.

After showing the worthlessness in trusting in "works of law" to save us, Paul then confidently announces that "Christ redeemed us from the curse of the law by becoming a curse for us." We don't need to rely on works of the law to save. We don't have to trust our own good deeds or fear the curse of God's law. Christ is sufficient for our salvation. He has bought us back from our slavery to the works of the law, which lead only to death and eternal bondage. His work on the cross delivers to us "the blessing given to Abraham" and "the promise of the Spirit."

See in this verse how Christ does it all. He "became a curse for us" — in the metaphor of the marketplace, Jesus Christ, God's Son, took our place as a slave on the auction block. "Christ redeemed us" — he is the one who paid the price for our freedom. And what was that price? Jesus himself was the price. "It was not with perishable things such as silver or gold that you were redeemed… but with the precious blood of Christ, a lamb without blemish or defect" (1 Peter 1:18-19). Christ is everything in the transaction: the redeemer, the slave standing in our place, and the ransom price with which we were bought.

Christ became a curse, but then that curse became a blessing for everyone on earth. Paul calls it "the blessing given to Abraham," but it is not for Abraham alone. It is the righteousness that comes by believing (v. 6). It is God's "not guilty" declaration over all people, (v. 8), and God's promises to the world made long ago through Abraham (v. 9).

The blessing given to Abraham comes to us "through Christ Jesus." The promise of the Spirit comes to us "by faith." We have the double gift of the Father, the blessing of redemption, given to us through the Son and the Spirit.

Although the picture of a slave market and the idea of "redemption" may not be as clear to us today as it was to the earliest Christians, we can still identify strongly with the feeling of "enslavement" that sin brings, and the joy that we have because Christ has "bought us back" from slavery and released us from sin's curse.

As redeemed and beloved former slaves, let us not sell ourselves back into slavery by allowing our sin to be our master. The door of our slave-wagon is standing wide open – let's not re-bar the door and let it cart us away to hell. Instead, let us be what God has made us: Redeemed!

Be What God Has Made You: Reconciled!

Once you were alienated from God and were enemies in your minds because of your evil behavior. But now he has reconciled you by Christ's physical body through death to present you holy in his sight, without blemish and free from accusation. (Colossians 1:21-22)

Sometimes, a concept is very hard to completely understand until we have a good understanding of its exact opposite. For example, we tend to take light for granted until we've felt the absolute darkness of a cave hundreds of feet below the earth's surface. We can't always appreciate God's blessing in providing us with food until we've felt the sharp pangs of real hunger. The trusted advice of a good friend is never more dear than right at the end of a period in which we have experienced profound loneliness. In the same way, the truth that we are reconciled to God is hard to appreciate without a discussion of its opposite: the fact that we were once completely alienated from him.

We often accept without question the fact that our society is separated and fragmented into countless sub-groups. People who live here are different from people who live over there. Those who speak one language are different from those who speak another language. Often, these separations take place along racial and ethnic lines, and they usually breed distrust, hostility, and violence. What should be a celebration of our God-given differences and an appreciation of our differing strengths becomes fertile ground for envy, suspicion, oppression, and even genocide.

These oh-so-human examples of alienation are only a faint clue to the vast, profound separation and alienation that exists between sinful people and the holy God. Our text for this week starts with a reminder of our former condition: we were "alienated from God," and "enemies... because of [our] evil behavior." Isaiah 59:2 reminds us, "Your iniquities have separated you from your God." Talk about alienation! It's not simply a multicultural question of "us vs. them" — it's a theological problem of "Him vs. us." And we're going to lose that fight every time. Our hostility toward God, and our alienation from him, aren't just a minor misunderstanding. They are a condemning divide that threatens to separate us from God forever in hell.

Many marriages end when the man and the woman, after some degree of work trying to save their marriage, decide to split up because of "irreconcilable differences." Whether their differences are truly unable to be resolved is, perhaps, a matter of debate, but one thing that can't be debated is that the separation, hostility and alienation that exists between us and God is humanly irreconcilable.

God, however, was not content to be alienated from the beloved people of his creation. Our text tells us that God has now "reconciled you by Christ's physical body through death." The death of Jesus on the cross ended the alienation and hostility that existed between us and God. In the words of Ephesians 2:16, Christ "reconciled [us] to God through the cross, by which he put to death [our] hostility." The alienation is over, the separation is ended. The hostilities have been called off. The two have again become one. We are reconciled to God.

On the cross, Christ called out, "My God, my God, why have you forsaken me?" (Mark 15:34). In that moment, Jesus was experiencing the ultimate alienation: separation from God and the torment of hell, an alienation that we deserved because of our sins. But in that moment, Jesus was also completing for us the ultimate reconciliation: through his death, we are made "holy in his sight, without blemish and free from accusation."

"All this is from God, who reconciled us to himself through Christ" (2 Corinthians 5:18). God has *reconciled* us — past tense. It's over and done, and has been for 2,000 years. God has reconciled us — he is the active subject, we are the passive objects. And it is, literally, a "cosmic" reconciliation: "God was reconciling *the world* to himself in Christ, not counting men's sins against them" (2 Corinthians 5:19).

The deeper, underlying, theological alienation between us and God has been removed by Christ. We are reconciled to God! Now the way is open for us to reconcile ourselves to one another. Let's not let racial, economic, social, geographic, ethnic or cultural barriers be an excuse for remaining alienated from our fellow human beings. We are reconciled! Let us be what God has made us. Let us "be reconciled" to each other (Matthew 5:24), just as in Christ God has reconciled us to himself.

Be What God Has Made You: At Peace!

Peace I leave with you; my peace I give you. I do not give to you as the world gives. Do not let your hearts be troubled and do not be afraid. (John 14:27)

"My peace I give you." This is one of Jesus' most famous, most powerful sayings. In times of strife, in times of trial, and in times of all-out war we cling to these words of our Savior and pray that his peace would be ours. But it's very interesting to consider the context in which Jesus said these words. Was he on a tranquil mountaintop, dispensing words of wisdom on living in harmony with everyone? Was he standing on a serene plateau next to the gently lapping waves of the Sea of Galilee, teaching seven surefire methods for reducing friction in interpersonal relationships? No. Jesus spoke these words of peace in an upper room in Jerusalem, on the night of his betrayal, at the beginning of the most heart-wrenching and violent twenty-four hours of his ministry.

The richly-textured Hebrew word for peace — *shalom* — has at its root the idea of entering into a state of wholeness and unity, of a restoration of harmony and a right relationship with someone.

This is the promise of God throughout Scripture. The Aaronic benediction of Numbers 6 says, "The LORD bless you and keep you; the LORD make his face shine upon you and be gracious to you; the LORD turn his face toward you and give you peace." The person who has God's peace is blessed, guarded, and treated graciously. Romans 5 promises, "Therefore, since we have been justified through faith, we have peace with God through our Lord Jesus Christ, through whom we have gained access by faith into this grace in which we now stand."

However, there is an intense paradox here: Jesus' peace comes through violence. In Matthew 10:34, Jesus warns, "Do not suppose that I have come to bring peace to the earth. I did not come to bring peace, but a sword." The Prince of Peace (Isaiah 6:9) is sent to earth on a violent mission: to crush the serpent's head (Genesis 3:15). Paul promises the Romans, "The God of peace will soon crush Satan under your feet" (16:20). *Crush* Satan, not negotiate a treaty with him.

Jesus' ministry itself was a preparation for a violent contest, ending in the violent death of the Son of God. "He then began to teach them that the Son of Man must suffer many things and be rejected... and that he must be killed" (Mark 8:31). Jesus suffered violence to bring us peace. In many ways, this is a good lesson for us survivors of the 20th century, who think that peace comes through negotiation, or conflict-resolution, or politically-correct policies of non-offense. Let me say it again:

Jesus' peace comes through violence — violence done to Jesus himself.

Our sin did violence to the relationship between us and God, and it took violence to end the conflict and restore peace. Jesus faced opposition all throughout his earthly ministry. He was arrested in the garden, and was cruelly treated at the hands of Jews and Romans alike. The peace, the state of wholeness and unity, that he had with the Father was ripped away as he was forsaken on Calvary's cross (Mark 15:34). Isaiah reminds us, "the punishment that brought us peace was upon him, and by his wounds we are healed" (Isaiah 53:5).

Jesus our Savior suffered violence for our sake. Nevertheless, his words of peace are true and eternal, and they apply to you and me the same as they applied to his first disciples that Maundy Thursday evening: "Peace I leave with you; my peace I give you. I do not give to you as the world gives."

We have peace with God. That peace is more than just a worldly "peace," the calm propping-up of our feet at the end of a busy day or a peace treaty between two hostile, warring nations. It's a restoration of harmony and a right relationship with our Holy Creator God. The enmity, the war, that began between us and God in the Garden of Eden has been ended. Our sinful mind was "hostile" to God (Romans 8:7), but God has made peace with us. That peace of God truly "transcends all understanding" and yet promises to "guard your hearts and your minds in Christ Jesus" (Philippians 4:7).

Since God has given us this peace, and since he has made us at peace with him, let us strive to live at peace with others too. God has promised us his peace and a right relationship with himself through Jesus Christ our Lord. Therefore, "let the peace of Christ rule in your hearts, since as members of one body you were called to peace" (Colossians 3:15). Let us be the agents of peace that God has called us to be. Let us be what God has made us!

Be What God Has Made You: A Free Slave!

Act as free people, but do not use your freedom as a cover-up to do wrong; instead, be God's slaves. (1 Peter 2:16, NET)

Jesus' peace comes to us through violence — a paradox of the first order, considered in the last devotion. This one is no less strange: we are called to be — and therefore we *are* — free slaves of God.

Free slaves? The phrase itself is a contradiction in terms. How do we understand this paradox? Is it possible to be both free and a slave? Do we ignore one and highlight the other? Do we blend them together in some lukewarm mush?

No! In the words of G. K. Chesterton, "Christianity got over the difficulty of combining furious opposites by keeping them both, and keeping them both furious."

First, remember the furious truth of what it is to be free in Christ. We are free from condemnation, free from the power of sin, and free from the slavery of the law. Like a prisoner with a "not guilty" verdict, we are acquitted before God's judgment bench because of Christ's sacrifice in our place (Romans 3:21-26). Like an addict, finally free from the clutching fingers of his addiction, we have thrown off the sin which so easily entangles to keep our eyes fixed on Jesus (Hebrews 12:1-2). And like a graduated senior who is finally free from the rules and demands of his former teachers, we are free from the caretaking regulations of the law to serve God in liberty (Galatians 3:24-25). We are truly free people in the Gospel because of Jesus' life, death, and resurrection.

Just as important, however, is the other half of the paradox. We need to furiously affirm our slavery. St. Paul tells the Galatians that Christ has indeed set them free, but in the very next breath he gives them instructions on how to use that freedom. He writes, "You, my brothers, were called to be free. But do not use your freedom to indulge the sinful nature; rather, serve one another in love" (Galatians 5:13). We are to use our freedom to serve [literally: be a slave to] one another. He wrote similar words to the Corinthians: "Though I am free and belong to no man, I make myself a slave to everyone, to win as many as possible… I have become all things to all men so that by all possible means I might save some. I do all this for the sake of the gospel, that I may share in its blessings" (1 Corinthians 9:19, 22-23). As furiously as we cling to our freedom in the Gospel, which is easy to do in America, we need to just as furiously cling to and remember our identity as slaves: first to God, and then to others.

Martin Luther explained our lives of free Christian service with these words:

A Christian is the most free lord of all, and subject to none. A Christian is the most dutiful servant of all, and subject to every one. Although these statements appear contradictory, yet, when they are found to agree together, they will make excellently for my purpose.

First, as regards kingship, every Christian is by faith so exalted above all things that, in spiritual power, he is completely lord of all things, so that nothing whatever can do him any hurt; yea, all things are subject to him, and are compelled to be subservient to his salvation.

[And yet], a man does not live for himself alone in this mortal body, in order to work on its account, but also for all people on earth; nay, he lives only for others, and not for himself. For it is to this end that he brings his own body into subjection, that he may be able to serve others more sincerely and more freely in all that he does; having nothing before his eyes but the necessities and the advantage of his neighbor.

Here is the truly Christian life, here is faith really working by love: when a man applies himself with joy and love to the works of that freest servitude in which he serves others voluntarily and for naught, himself abundantly satisfied in the fullness and riches of his own faith.

In Mel Gibson's Revolutionary War epic *The Patriot*, Benjamin Martin is a wealthy farmer who opens his home as a makeshift field hospital after a bloody battle. As he is tending the wounded soldiers, a cruel British officer, Colonel Tavington, rides up to the farmhouse. Tavington has the American wounded shot on the spot. He then orders Martin's house burned as punishment for harboring the enemy. Before riding away, the evil Dragoon commander turns to a group of black field hands and says, "By order of His Majesty, King George III, all slaves of rebellious colonists will be freed in exchange for service in His Majesty's Army."

A grizzled old slave looks up at the pompous Tavington and says, "We ain't slaves. We work here of our own accord."

May we, who have been saved by Christ's free service to us, also have such an attitude. May we gladly be God's free slaves. May our lives be lives of free service to our Lord and Savior, Jesus Christ, and to those people whom he has given us to serve.

✠

Be What God Has Made You: A Living Sacrifice!

Therefore, I urge you, brothers, in view of God's mercy, to offer your bodies as living sacrifices, holy and pleasing to God—this is your spiritual act of worship. (Romans 12:1)

Often, when a section of Scripture begins with the word "therefore," it's important to look back and see the connection the author is making with what came before. For example, Christ's Great Commission in Matthew 28:19-20 begins with the word "therefore." (Therefore go and make disciples of all nations...) Now look at the verse just before the "therefore" — "Jesus came to them and said, 'All authority in heaven and on earth has been given to me. Therefore go...'" See the important connection? Jesus, by virtue of his status as God's Son, and in the victorious exaltation of his Resurrection, has all authority in heaven and on earth; therefore his command carries divine authority and confers on us the power to fulfill that Commission as his ambassadors on earth.

Today's verse also begins with a "therefore" which is easy to miss (it's only 3 letters long in Greek), and yet contains a wealth of meaning. In fact, when we look backwards to try to see exactly what Paul is referring to with his "therefore," we can easily come to the conclusion that he is referring to the entire letter up to this point. The first word of chapter 12 seems to be a fulcrum, a turning point, in the whole epistle, as Paul goes from foundational truths about sin (chapters 1-2), justification by faith (chapters 3-5), new life and salvation (chapter 6), deliverance from the law (chapter 7), guidance from the Spirit (chapter 8), and God's righteousness in spite of man's unbelief (chapters 9-11) and moves to practical application of those truths in details about life in the community of believers (chapter 12), life as Christians in the world (chapter 13), guidelines for dealing with weaker brothers in the faith (chapters 14-15) and some more personal matters (chapter 16).

And so, on the basis of everything he has said so far in the book of Romans, and in preparation for everything he is about to say, Paul encourages us to "offer our bodies as living sacrifices." Right away we recognize yet another paradox in our calling as Christians. Like the peace of Jesus that comes through violence, and the freedom God gives us to be his slaves, the idea of "living sacrifice" is paradoxical. The word Paul uses for "sacrifice" is the word for an animal that is slain and burnt up in smoke (see Leviticus 1). And yet we are to be living sacrifices. What does Paul mean by this?

One commentator explains, "Here there is a strong paradox: our bodies are to be presented like those of the animals — not like them to be slain, yet like them to be made God's so completely that during our whole life we are as good as slain." This is, in fact, what it means to be "holy" — that is, consecrated, set apart, and devoted to God. Stated another way, we are "dead to sin but alive to God in Christ Jesus" (Romans 6:11). We are further told, "You are not your own; you were bought at a price. Therefore honor God with your body" (1 Corinthians 6:19-20).

I am reminded of the famous quotation by twentieth-century Christian martyr Jim Elliot: "He is no fool who gives what he cannot keep to gain that which he cannot lose." To be a living sacrifice is to live our entire life as if we had already given that life to God, unconcerned about our present because our future is so secure. In the words of Paul, "to live is Christ and to die is gain" (Philippians 1:21).

However, there are times when, in spite of God's mercies (rather than "in view of" them), that we just don't feel like sacrificing ourselves. One wise guy observed, "the problem with living sacrifices is that they keep trying to crawl off the altar." In those times of doubt and half-hearted obedience, let us fix our eyes on Jesus, who did not shirk from his own appointed self-sacrifice (Hebrews 12:2), but instead gave himself fully to his Father's will (Matthew 26:39). This he did not merely to be our *example*, but to be our *substitute*, and to exchange his perfect, holy life for our sinful, corrupted one.

Once again, it is important to remember that we are not being commanded to do something that

God has not already done for us in Christ. We are called to offer our bodies as living sacrifices, while Christ in his mercy is the perfect Living Sacrifice for us. He offered his body as a sacrifice on the cross (Philippians 2:8) and yet rose from the dead by the power of God and lives and rules eternally (Ephesians 1:19-20). We are not being ordered to muster up the courage to make the long walk towards the altar of sacrifice alone. Instead, "in view of God's mercy," we are called to spiritual worship of God. We are called to be what God has made us in Christ Jesus. Like Jesus, we are sacrificed and yet live — in fact, we are sacrificed and yet live because of Jesus.

Part Two:
Your Relationship to Yourself

Be What God Has Made You: A New Creation!

Therefore, if anyone is in Christ, he is a new creation; the old has gone, the new has come! (2 Corinthians 5:17)

In the last section of the book, we considered our relationship to God. We saw that God has made us his children, alive with him, free from condemnation, righteous, redeemed, reconciled, at peace, free slaves, and living sacrifices. Look at all of the things that God has made us in Christ! Through Jesus, we have a relationship with God himself. He took what we destroyed through our sin and re-created it (and us) in Christ, restoring our relationship with God himself.

In this second section, we now look at our relationship to ourselves. As Christians, how do we relate to ourselves? What is our "self-image" now that we have this new relationship to God? If it is true that "it is no longer I who live, but Christ who lives in me" (Galatians 2:20), what, exactly, does that make *me*?

The first part of our relationship with ourselves on which we're going to focus is that, in Christ, we are a new creation. Let's take an in-depth look at this verse.

In English, we usually use the phrase "if anyone" in a slightly doubtful way, as if we're not sure we're going to encounter someone that fits the qualification. "If anyone on the plane is a doctor, we need them to come to the front." The way this phrase is used in this verse, though, is a little more optimistic. It's more like saying "whoever," or "anyone who." "Anyone who ordered a shirt can pick it up in the lobby." So, "whoever is in Christ is a new creation." There's no limiting "if," as if we're doubting that anyone might be in Christ. It's a joyous proclamation of the truth about all who are in Christ.

What, then, does it mean to be "in Christ"? That question is deeper than we can possibly know. Adolf Deissmann, a German theologian in the early 20th century, compared being "in Christ" to the air we breathe. The atmosphere is all around us. It surrounds us and envelops us. Everywhere we go, there it is. Further, even as we are in the air, the air is also fully in us, filling our lungs and permeating every cell in our body with life-giving oxygen. So it is to be "in Christ." "In him we live and move and have our being" (Acts 17:28). We are fully immersed in him and his love, and every fiber of our being is permeated with his life-giving grace.

Similarly, Nicholas Cabasilas, a fourteenth-century Byzantine theologian, compared our life in Christ to a room that is completely filled with rays of sunlight streaming in through an open window. By itself, the room is dark and cold. But in Christ, there is light and life. In the same way we are infused, or shot through, with divine light and life through our connection to Christ.

There's more. Being "in Christ" also indicates a deeply-seated change of allegiance. At one time we were "sold as a slave to sin" (Romans 7:14), but we have traded the harsh taskmasters of sin, death and the devil for allegiance to Christ as our Lord by faith.

Being "in Christ" means being a citizen of his kingdom, pitching our tents within his borders. Professor Michael Gorman, looking at the 90+ times that the phrase "in Christ" appears in the New Testament, writes, "to be 'in Christ' principally means to be under the influence of Christ's power, especially the power to be conformed to him and his cross, by participation in the life of a community that acknowledges his lordship." (There's a lot in that last statement!)

After identifying us as "in Christ," Paul then calls us "new." The Greek word he uses for "new" has the idea of being "unused; new in quality; good-as-new." We're not talking about a wet-behind the ears "new" college grad or a "brand-new" but bottom-of-the-line import car — this "new" is the "new" we would use to talk about a '57 Chevy in perfect mint condition that had been lovingly restored by a master mechanic.

We were created in God's image, stamped like coins with the likeness of God himself. But through our own personal sin, we have worn that image away into an unrecognizable blur on a shabby slug of metal. The good news is that "in

Christ," those coins have been re-minted with a freshly-stamped image of the King. We are *new*.

Finally, it's important to note that Paul here calls us "creations." A creation is made by the creator, without any input or cooperation from us. We are God's handiwork (see Ephesians 2:10, and again, note the "in Christ Jesus"!) created to do good works.

What does all of this mean? We are in Christ. Our past is gone. Our old status is no more. Our old sins do not control us any longer. We have a fresh start. More than just a blanket "forgiveness" for our sins, we have a whole new life. A new purpose, new focus, new direction — a new identity as a new creation of God in Christ. "Therefore, if anyone is in Christ, he is a new creation; the old has gone, the new has come!" Let us be what God has made us: new creations!

Be What God Has Made You: Confident in the Faith!

Now it is God who has made us for this very purpose and has given us the Spirit as a deposit, guaranteeing what is to come. Therefore we are always confident and know that as long as we are at home in the body we are away from the Lord. We live by faith, not by sight. We are confident, I say, and would prefer to be away from the body and at home with the Lord. (2 Corinthians 5:5-8)

Confidence is an interesting thing. It's important for us to have confidence, and yet it is even more important that the thing in which we have confidence be worthy of our trust. It's important that I trust my brakes to stop my car; without that confidence, I won't be a safe driver (and I might not drive at all). But, obviously, it's even more important that my brakes actually stop my car. If they don't, all my trust is worthless.

The same thing is true of our faith, which is "being sure of what we hope for and certain of what we do not see" (Hebrews 11:1). It's important for us to have confidence in God, and important for us to believe the promises he has given us. Without that confidence, we are essentially calling

God a liar (and might not be Christians at all). But, obviously, it's even more important that God is actually trustworthy. If he's not, then "our preaching is useless and so is your faith" (1 Corinthians 15:14).

"But Christ has indeed been raised from the dead!" St. Paul proclaims. (1 Corinthians 15:20). God is trustworthy. All of his promises are "Yes" in Christ (2 Corinthians 1:20). "We know that the one who raised the Lord Jesus from the dead will also raise us with Jesus and present us with you in his presence" (2 Corinthians 4:14). The Bible — and our own lives! — are full of testimony that our Lord is "Faithful and True" (Revelation 19:11).

In times of trial, struggle, and doubt, then, what is a Christian to do? Look to himself, or look to his God? Stated like that, the answer seems obvious — but how many times have we done the opposite? How many times do we try to increase our faith by looking at our faith, instead of looking to our faithful God and his unfailing Word?

I came into the profession of teaching by something of a back door. I was almost totally unprepared to be in front of a classroom, and my first week of teaching was nothing short of disastrous. It's probably not overstatement to say that these words (posted on the bulletin board over my desk) saved my teaching career, as God used them to take my eyes off of myself and my day-to-day struggles and re-focus my confidence where it belonged:

> I know that the God of all mercy has called me to his eternal glory, unto which he chose

me in Christ Jesus before the foundation of the world, and I am certain that he will keep me firm unto the end, unto the entrance into the eternal kingdom of our Lord Jesus Christ.

Whence comes this blessed firmness and certainty for me? From some special revelation concerning God's secret counsel? No; but from the common revelation of the divine will of grace in the Gospel of Jesus Christ in whom I believe.

Because I know in whom I believe, namely in the God who has saved me and called me with a Holy Calling according to his own purpose and grace, therefore I am persuaded that he is able to guard that which I have committed unto him against that day.

When the God of all grace perfects, establishes, strengthens me in faith, then is my calling and election sure.

In short, our calling, election, and salvation are sure because God says they are, and we can be confident in God's promises because God is trustworthy. That kind of confidence really does have an effect on how we think about ourselves. We don't have to count on ourselves or our own abilities. We don't have to worry that we might mess things up — don't worry, we will. We don't buy into the world's idea of "self-confidence," because we know that our self is a pretty stupid thing to have confidence in.

Even more importantly, our faith stops being about ourselves and returns again and again to the foot of the cross, to behold Christ in our place, living and dying for us. The certainty of our salvation does not rest on the strength of our faith, or the holiness of our walk, or the depth of our theological insight. Our certainty and confidence for salvation rests squarely on the certain and trustworthy shoulders of Jesus of Nazareth.

And so, instead of falling to the temptation to rely on ourselves to get things done, or accomplish something meaningful, or stand firm in faith until the end, we learn about our limitations in every aspect of life, learn to accept them, and begin to trust more and more on Christ. We live by faith, not by sight.

God has given us his Holy Spirit as a deposit, a guarantee of what is to come. We know, by faith, that someday we will be at home with the Lord. In the meantime, while we are in the body, in our relationship to ourselves, let us be what God has made us — confident in the faith.

Be What God Has Made You: An Imitator of God!

Be imitators of God, therefore, as dearly loved children, and live a life of love, just as Christ loved us and gave himself up for us as a fragrant offering and sacrifice to God. (Ephesians 5:1,2)

"Imitation," they say, "is the sincerest form of flattery." God hardly needs our flattery, but just like a son who loves and respects his father so much that he wants to do whatever daddy does, we look at our Father in heaven and want to be more like him. We are called to be imitators of God.

What qualities of God are we to imitate? Clearly, we've already dropped the ball on omniscience. Omnipotence is right out, too, as we struggle with our weaknesses and tumble exhausted into bed at night. We can't imitate God's perfect justice, either — in fact, Jesus tells us not to when he says, "do not judge" (Luke 6:37). We are not to avenge injustice, which is something God reserves for himself (Deuteronomy 32:35). Even the venerable question "What Would Jesus Do?" can sometimes lead us astray — after all, when confronted by hungry people, Jesus miraculously made bread. Faced with a dry party, he made a hundred gallons of wine. Faced with unjust accusations, torture, and death, he submitted without a word. What Jesus did in a particular situation isn't always appropriate for us to try to do, and it can be blasphemous to assume otherwise.

So, how are we to imitate God? Simply, by love. Paul tells us, "Live a life of love, just as Christ loved us." The Apostle John reminds us that "God is love" (1 John 4:8). Love is the ultimate imitation of God. "Love is the fulfillment of the law" (Romans 13:10). The way we show that we are his disciples is when we "love one another" (John 13:35) as "he first loved us" (1 John 4:19). Jesus told us, "Greater love has no one than this, that he lay down his life for his friends" (John 15:13), and then he "showed the full extent of his love" (John 13:1) by dying on Calvary's cross for us, his friends. We are probably not going to be called to imitate Christ by dying on a literal cross, but we are called to "take up [our] cross" (Luke 9:23), just as he did. We are to imitate God by loving.

But there is a problem with all of this. The self-giving, sacrificial love of God is very hard to imitate. So hard, in fact, that it is impossible for us to truly be imitators of God. After all, the love of God is called, "perfect love" (1 John 4:18), and no matter how we might, occasionally, feel and show truly unselfish love to others, the love that we muster up in ourselves can hardly be considered "perfect." The perfect example of Christ's love is something far above our own ability to imitate. The real question, then, isn't a pious and academic, "How can we better imitate God?" but rather a desperate and humble, "What happens to us when we can't imitate God?"

The answer to that question is found in the verse right before our text, and is pointed back to by another *therefore*: "...in Christ God forgave you" (Ephesians 4:32).

"In Christ, God forgave you." God's forgiveness in Christ is a past action that has ongoing effect in our lives. God's forgiveness is not contingent on anything: not our good deeds, our faithfulness, or our ability to imitate him. God's forgiveness in Christ is absolute and absolutely true. As the saying goes, there is nothing we can do to make God love us more, and there is nothing we can do to make God love us less. Not even our weak, humble, imperfect attempts at imitating him have any effect on his forgiving grace and mercy shown to us in Jesus Christ our Savior. "He does not treat us as our sins deserve" (Psalm 103:10), but "gave himself up for us as a... sacrifice to God."

Therefore, confident in our relationship with the Father, in the Son, through the Holy Spirit, we live a life of love in imitation of God. We don't imitate God like an employee sucking up to his boss trying to get a promotion. We don't imitate God like a student on the playground trying to fit in with the cool kids. We imitate God as dearly loved children who are trying to show love and respect to their dear *Abba*, Father.

Finally, remember this: we are able to be imitators of God, and to be like him, only insofar as Jesus became like us. To paraphrase St. Athanasius of Alexandria, "The Son of God became like us, so that we might become like him." Peter tells us, "he has given us his very great and precious promises, so that through them you may *participate in the divine nature*" (2 Peter 1:4). Likewise, in 1 John 3:2 we read that "we will be like him." Talk about imitating God!

In his great love, God sent his Son to become a human being, so that by grace, we human beings could be imitators of God — imperfectly in this world, and perfectly in glory in the world to come. Let us be what God has made us, and imitate God as we live lives of love by his grace.

Be What God Has Made You: Able To Do Everything!

I can do everything through him who gives me strength. (Philippians 4:13)

I don't know about you, but I've always liked this verse. It really makes me feel safe and secure, and sort of validates the American Dream ideal that "you can do anything you set your mind to." It's also a great comfort to me when I'm faced with trials or troubles that come into my life. I can do everything through him — what words of promise!

But I've also been getting more confused by it. As life goes on, I've begun to get the sneaking suspicion that I really can't do everything, no matter how much I put my mind to it. There will be no leaping of tall buildings in a single bound. I will never, ever, take a puck drop in Game 7 of the Stanley Cup Finals. I might indeed learn something new every day, but that new thing is often a discovery of yet another limitation of my weak flesh. So how is it that Paul can so confidently say, "I can do everything"?

This verse from Paul is similar to some of Jesus' perplexing statements about prayer and faith. In

John 14:14, Jesus promises, "You may ask me for anything in my name, and I will do it." And yet, even if we use the magic words, "in your name," the prayer for the Ferrari still goes unanswered.

How can Jesus confidently promise, "If you believe, you will receive whatever you ask for in prayer." (Matthew 21:22)? Are our unanswered prayers evidence of too much doubt in our life? Does the fact that we can't "do everything" mean that we don't have saving faith in Jesus?

Not at all! When we pray for something "in faith," that doesn't mean that the outcome of our prayer is a measure of our faith in Jesus, and if our prayer isn't answered it means we're not believers. Remember that faith has to have an object, a promise of God in which to trust.

To pray "in faith" simply means to pray with trust in a specific promise of God. We often wonder why we can't throw mountains into the sea (Mark 11:23), but the answer is clear: God has never promised to answer our prayer that a mountain be thrown into the sea. That is not a prayer "in Jesus' name" (even if we tack those words onto the end of it) because it is not in line with God's will and promises revealed to us in the Bible. As Professor Seigbert Becker reminds us, "Where there is no promise, there can be no faith."

But where God has promised something, we are encouraged — even commanded — to lay hold of those promises in faith and to ask for them earnestly in prayer. A prayer of faith in Jesus' name — made in accord with God's promises, with humble submission to God's will (not ours) — will always be answered. And no promise is more sure or certain in Scripture than that God loves us and has saved us by uniting us with Jesus in his life, death, and resurrection. So when we pray for the spiritual blessings that God has promised to us in Christ, we can be certain that God hears and answers us.

In the same way, we can do everything that is in accord with God's will. Remember, we do it "though him." It is God who blesses us with the strength to carry out his will in this world. It is God who gives us the strength to overcome the trials and adversities in our life. It is God who "arms me with strength, and makes my way perfect" (Psalm 18:32). And is God who often withholds strength from us when we attempt to do things that are against his will (much like he chooses not to answer prayers for Ferraris and mountain-moving).

The *Apology of the Augsburg Confession*, one of the foundational documents of the Lutheran Church, says this about faith: "Faith justifies and saves, not on the ground that it is a work in itself worthy, but only because *it receives the promised mercy*." In other words, faith doesn't save — it is the object of our faith, Jesus Christ, who saves.

So, no. Maybe we can't leap tall buildings in a single bound. Maybe we can't get down on our knees and pray for a Ferrari "in Jesus' name" and wake up the next morning to find one in the garage. Maybe we can't do "everything" that our human flesh would like to be able to do.

But God's Word is sure. The "promised mercy" that we receive in faith is greater and more impressive than a Ferrari. The "everything" that we can do through God who strengthens us is greater and more impressive than uprooting geological features and winning hockey games. God, in his strength, has made us "able to do everything" through faith in Jesus our Lord. Cling to his sure and certain promises.

Be What God Has Made You: Strong in His Mighty Power!

Finally, be strong in the Lord and in his mighty power. (Ephesians 6:10)

This verse encourages us to "be strong." But how can we, as weak and fallen human beings, ever truly be strong? What does it mean to be strong in the Lord? For our answers, let's consider two saints of old: the Apostle Paul and the Virgin Mary.

Paul knew better than any of us how weak we are as sinful and fallen human beings. After pleading with the Lord in prayer three times for the weakness of his so-called thorn in the flesh to be removed, Paul received his answer from the Lord Jesus himself: "My grace is sufficient for you, for my power is made perfect in weakness." However, even after receiving this "no" answer, Paul concludes: "Therefore I will boast all the more gladly about my weaknesses, so that Christ's power may rest on me. That is why, for Christ's sake, I delight in weaknesses, in insults, in hardships, in persecutions, in difficulties. For when I am weak, then I am strong" (2 Corinthians 12:9-10).

God's strength and power do not look like human strength and power. In fact, they look quite a bit like weakness. An unassuming paperback book in the bedside table of a rat-trap hotel is "the gospel, [which] is the power of God for the salvation of all who believe" (Romans 1:16). A crucified Jew, bleeding and dying in public shame on a Roman cross, is God in the flesh — "Christ the power of God" (1 Corinthians 1:24). The Lord's strength is not what we would expect, but it is infinitely more.

Graham Tomlin, in his book *The Power of the Cross: Theology and the Death of Christ in Paul, Luther and Pascal*, explains the difference between God's strength and what human beings consider to be strong:

> God gets things done not by a conventional human use of power, by displays of force, impressive signs, or sophisticated wisdom. He achieves salvation through an act of what to human eyes is powerlessness on the cross; he chooses to dwell in Corinth in a group of 'nothings' in the eyes of Corinthian society; he creates these new communities through the preaching of an unimpressive artisan tentmaker.

When we are weak and humbly admit it, we quietly lay aside all of our efforts to do things ourselves and trust God to make us strong in his own way. The expression, "if you want something done right, do it yourself" sort of misses the mark.

When we really want something done right, we look to the Lord and his mighty power.

The Virgin Mary knew very well what having the Lord's strength meant in her daily life. In her song, the *Magnificat*, she praises God with these words (Luke 1:46-55):

> My soul glorifies the Lord and my spirit rejoices in God my Savior, for he has been mindful of the humble state of his servant. From now on all generations will call me blessed, for the Mighty One has done great things for me — holy is his name. His mercy extends to those who fear him, from generation to generation. He has performed mighty deeds with his arm; he has scattered those who are proud in their inmost thoughts. He has brought down rulers from their thrones but has lifted up the humble. He has filled the hungry with good things but has sent the rich away empty. He has helped his servant Israel, remembering to be merciful to Abraham and his descendants forever, even as he said to our fathers.

Look at Mary's words. See how God acts with power and strength on behalf of the weak, the humble, and the poor. We are strong in the Lord. But don't forget: the mightiest deed that God will do, as he sweeps Satan from his throne forever, will look like the ultimate act of weakness in human history.

So how can we be strong in the Lord? By humbly recognizing our weakness and looking to God in faith; by meeting him regularly in his Word; and by exercising spiritual discipline with the Lord's mighty power. A word about "spiritual disciplines:"

Frederica Matthewes-Greene observes that weightlifters don't pump iron in case someday they should happen upon a crowd gathered in dismay around a barbell. Rather, they exercise to strengthen their bodies for athletic competition and hard physical work. Likewise, we do not pursue spiritual disciplines like worship, prayer, reading Scripture, and "quiet time" so that we can win a Bible read-a-thon. We don't fast to prepare for the day when the store is out of our favorite kind of muffin. No. We practice self-discipline so that, in the Lord's mighty power and through our connection to him in the Word, we will have strength to fight temptation in the "real world." Like the Apostle Paul, we beat our bodies and make them our slaves so that through God's mighty power we "will not be disqualified from the prize" (1 Corinthians 9:27).

We are strong in the Lord, and in his mighty power. Let us sing with Moses, "The LORD is my strength and my song; he has become my salvation." (Exodus 15:2).

✠

Be What God Has Made You: A Jar of Clay!

For we do not preach ourselves, but Jesus Christ as Lord, and ourselves as your servants for Jesus' sake. For God, who said, "Let light shine out of darkness," made his light shine in our hearts to give us the light of the knowledge of the glory of God in the face of Christ. But we have this treasure in jars of clay to show that this all-surpassing power is from God and not from us. (2 Corinthians 4:5-7)

The Latin word ego, which came into English thanks to Sigmund Freud, means simply "I" or "I, myself." Over the years, the term has come to mean (with a negative connotation) the opinion we have about ourselves. In this section of our theme for this book, we have been talking about our ego — our relationship to ourselves.

How should we think about ourselves? The first word we usually think of is "humility." The Bible tells us that we are not to think of ourselves more highly than we ought (Romans 12:3). Ephesians 4:2 reminds us to be "completely humble." James even gives this seemingly paradoxical advice: "The brother in humble circumstances ought to take pride in his high position" (1:9).

All that we have is a gracious gift of God. The credit for everything we are or do goes to the Lord, as James again writes, "Every good and perfect gift is from above, coming down from the Father of the heavenly lights" (James 1:17). Our self-esteem is not based on accomplishing our goals. Our self-image is not based on what other people think of us. Our self-worth is not based on how productive we are, how much money we can earn, how many people know us, or even how successful our children become.

A Biblical view of ego always contains a healthy realism (one might even say "skepticism") about our natural condition as fallen humans, and a humble acknowledgement that all that we are and have is a result of "Christ who lives in [us]" (Galatians 2:20), and not anything we can do on our own.

On the side of a desert mountain overlooking the cities of El Paso, Texas and Juarez, Mexico is a message, spelled out in white-painted rocks big enough to be seen by over three million people: "LA BIBLIA ES LA VERDAD. LÉALA." The Bible is the truth. Read it. Obviously, that message was put there by human beings. But it still looks strangely like God himself bent down from heaven and wrote a quick memo to his people, reminding us in the hustle of our workaday commute of the "one thing needed" (Luke 10:42).

If only the rest of God's messages came that way, unmistakably inscribed on the bedrock or traced across the sky in letters of fire. How many people would think twice about skipping church on Sunday if a heavenly alarm clock/trumpet shook them out of their beds? How many skeptics would still continue to doubt the miracle of the Resurrection if the risen Christ intervened personally and visibly in everyone's life, just like he did for the Pharisee Saul (Acts 9)? Yes, it's true that "the heavens declare the glory of God" (Psalm 19:1), but it's also sadly true that people are more than capable of ignoring God's self-revelation in nature to turn to idolatry and unbelief (see Romans 1).

Well, then, if it's not heavenly graffiti on a mountainside or a voice from the clouds at 10:30 a.m. every Sunday morning, how is God's truth revealed? How has God seen fit to pass on the "treasure" of the "glory of God in the face of Christ"? Simple: through us.

Before his Ascension, Jesus commissioned his followers to "go and make disciples" (Matthew 28:19). He didn't stay to do it himself. He passed that job on to his people.

Why would God do this? Why would he trust the ministry of the Gospel to simple, sinful, weak, fallible human beings? Why wouldn't he give the job to a legion of angels? Why wouldn't he just do it himself? I'm sure he could do a better job than the most eloquent preacher, or the most brilliant seminary professor, or the most mediocre devotion-writer. Why trust such an important job to such unreliable workers?

I have no idea. But he has.

The same God who created all the light in the universe put the light of faith in our hearts by the power of the Holy Spirit working through the Gospel — a Gospel that was taught to us by another human being, just as weak and fallible as we are. That person heard from another, and that person from another, and so on. One clay jar pouring out the knowledge of the glory of God into other clay jars, who in turn fill other clay jars.

We are jars of clay that hold an invaluable treasure. God has given us a task, and he has given us the means to accomplish it. Let us humbly consider what that means about us, and also what it means about God. Let us be what God has made us.

✠

Be What God Has Made You: Dead to Sin!

He himself bore our sins in his body on the tree, so that we might die to sins and live for righteousness. (1 Peter 2:24)

What a difference a couple of letters can make. Think of the difference between wishing someone a "Merry Christmas" and wishing them a "Sorry Christmas." Only two letters are different, but what a change in meaning! In Spanish, students often miss the distinction between *nueve* (nine), *nieve* (snow), *nuevo* (new), and *novio* (boyfriend) with humorous results. To me, though, the most theologically significant difference that the exchange of two English letters can produce is the difference between being "dead *in* sin" and being "dead *to* sin."

"Dead *in* sin" is our spiritual starting point. St. Paul reminds us that we were "dead in our transgressions and sins… gratifying the cravings of our sinful nature and… by nature objects of wrath" (Ephesians 2:1-3). We were physically alive and able to move around, but spiritually dead and unable to take even the first, tiniest step toward God. "Dead in sin" means "powerless to help ourselves." It took God's action to make us "alive in Christ" (Colossians 2:13), because dead men cannot resurrect themselves.

"Dead *to* sin," however, is a completely different matter. When you are "dead to" something, that thing isn't important to you anymore. It doesn't factor into your thinking. We are "dead to sin" — that means that sin no longer has the power to control us. We no longer live under sin's tyranny. In 1 Corinthians we are reminded that "The sting of death is sin, and the power of sin is the law" (15:56). But neither death nor sin nor the law has any power to condemn us, because God "has given us the victory through our Lord Jesus Christ" (15:57).

Our old self, the sinful self which has been dead in sin since birth, was killed with Christ on Calvary's cross. "For we know that our old self was crucified with [Christ] so that the body of sin might be done away with, that we should no longer be slaves to sin" (Romans 6:6). Christ's death, which was also our death, killed the sin that was controlling us, so that we are now dead to sin.

Pastor Don Matzat wrote a book called *Christ Esteem: Where the Search for Self-Esteem Ends*. In it, he encourages Christians to die to self, to get their focus off of self and on to Christ. He reminds us over and over that we do not *have* a problem; rather, we *are* the problem. Then he writes:

> If I am the problem, what is the solution? If you educate me, you will get a smart sinner. If you discipline me, you will get a disciplined sinner. If you refine me, I become a re-

fined sinner. If you give me more religion, I will be a religious sinner. Whatever you do with me, you cannot change what I am, and what I am is the problem.

So what is the solution? The gospel of Jesus Christ. Matzat continues:

> The call of the gospel is away from self and onto Jesus, because self is the problem and Jesus is the solution... We will not understand the meaning of, nor grasp in faith the new life offered in Christ, until we are willing to pass the same judgment upon ourselves that God has already passed upon us through the cross. The death of Jesus Christ passed total, complete judgment upon everything that we are, everything we have done regardless of whether it is good or bad, and everything we possess. Because Jesus died, we are dead! We have been cancelled out by the cross.

We are dead; "dead to sin but alive to God in Christ Jesus" (Romans 6:11). We are freed from the burden of "self" — of sin and selfishness — so that we "might die to sins and live for righteousness."

Notice the double substitution here. We aren't just dead to something old. We are also alive to something new. In Ephesians 4, we see the same pattern emerging: not this, but that. Paul instructs his readers to "put off your old self... and to put on the new self" (22-24). We are to "put off falsehood" and "speak truthfully" (25). We "must steal no longer, but must work... to share with those in need" (28). We are to cease "unwholesome talk," and replace it with "what is helpful for building others up" (29). And we are to "get rid of all bitterness, rage and anger, brawling and slander" so that we may "be kind and compassionate to one another" (31-32). Not this, but that. Dead to sin, but alive to God. God replaces our old sinful way of life with a brand new life in Christ.

Paul tells the Colossians, "You died, and your life is now hidden with Christ in God… Put to death, therefore, whatever belongs to your earthly nature: sexual immorality, impurity, lust, evil desires and greed, which is idolatry" (Colossians 3:3-5). Because of our death to sin, we can also put to death the deeds that flow from the sin within us.

All of this stuff about being "dead to sin" would be easier to believe, I suppose, if we could, for even one minute, actually stop sinning. But we know we can't. We know we will sin every day of our lives. On this side of heaven, we are *simul justus et peccator* — sinner and saint at the same time. But God promises it, and we grab hold of his promises in faith. Believe it when God says that you are "dead to sin" because of Christ's death, and that you are "alive to God" because of Christ's resurrection. Rejoice in who you are in Christ. By his power, be what God has made you!

✠

Part Three:
Your Relationship to Other Believers

Be What God Has Made You:
A Living Stone in a Spiritual House!

As you come to him, the living Stone—rejected by men but chosen by God and precious to him — you also, like living stones, are being built into a spiritual house to be a holy priesthood, offering spiritual sacrifices acceptable to God through Jesus Christ. (1 Peter 2:4,5)

As we enter into the third section of our book, let's take a minute to look at our overall theme, *Be What God Has Made You*, and review the ground we've covered so far. We've been reflecting on the identity that God has given to us — taking a close look at who we are in Jesus Christ. During the first part of the book, we looked at the most important relationship we have: our relationship to God. Then, in the second section, we looked at our relationship to ourselves — what does our changed standing with God mean to us as individuals? Now, in this third part, we move away from ourselves and into our relationship with other Christians. How do we interact with others who share our identity as children of God and believers in Jesus?

The first metaphor of our life together in Christ that we will explore is that of "living stones." One of the most interesting things about this particular picture, to me, is who is using it: the Apostle Peter, also known as Cephas, of whom Jesus once said, "I tell you that you are Peter, and on this rock I will build my church, and the gates of Hades will not overcome it" (Matthew 16:18). Now Peter is using the same picture to point to Christ the "living Stone" and remind his readers that they, like him, are living stones.

But of course, believers are not literal pieces of rock. Nor are we each so solid and certain in our subjective faith that we deserve to be called "stones." No, we are stones because of the rock-solid *object* of our faith: Jesus Christ. It was not Peter's own personal conviction that earned him praise from Jesus. Rather, it was his confession of the true and objective fact that Jesus of Nazareth is, indeed, "the Christ, the Son of the living God" (Matthew 16:16). In the same way, each of us has been made spiritually alive by the "life-giving spirit" of God (1 Corinthians 15:45) to be "living stones" in the image of Christ himself, and can confess that fact with the same certainty with which Peter did.

Now, look again at the picture that Peter uses of us as believers. We are not just individual living stones, all lying in a field somewhere; some close, some far, all scattered. We are "being built into a spiritual house." We are more than just individual believers in this world. We are being joined together by our Maker into something that's more than just the sum of its parts. Each of us has a place in this spiritual house. All of us depend on each other. And we all depend on Christ, the Living Cornerstone.

As we consider our relationship to other believers, then, we need to remember the concept of *community*. One stone, one individual believer, is never alone. It's not just "me 'n' Jesus." There is always a sharing of what all Christians jointly have in common: "one Lord, one faith, one baptism" (Ephesians 4:5). Furthermore, church is more than just a bunch of individuals who happen to believe the same things getting together on Sunday mornings. We are an organic, inter-dependent fellowship, whose unity is essentially the same as the relationship between Jesus and the Father (John 17:21).

But this idea of fellowship with other believers (community) and continuity with those who came before us in faith (tradition) is becoming lost in American churches today. It seems we have absorbed a bit too much of the American ideal of the rugged individualist, free and independent of outside authority. Nancy Pearcy, the author of *Total Truth: Liberating Christianity from its Cultural Captivity*, writes: "In many churches, the individual alone with his Bible is regarded as the core of Christian life." Then she quotes sociologist Wade Clark Roof, who observes, "The real story of American religious life in this half-century is *the rise of a new sovereign self* that defines and sets limits on the very meaning of the divine." A far cry from St. Peter's words, and a far cry from the biblical reality of our common identity as God's spiritual house.

We have Christ's own promise that that spiritual house, the Church, will not be overcome by the gates of hell. We know that as a community of believers, called out from the world as Christ's Church, our foundation is sure and cannot be shaken. Listen to St. Paul's classic words on the subject:

> "He came and preached peace to you who were far away and peace to those who were near. For through him we both have access to the Father by one Spirit. Consequently, you are no longer foreigners and aliens, but fellow citizens with God's people and members of God's household, built on the foundation of the apostles and prophets, with Christ Jesus himself as the chief cornerstone. In him the whole building is joined together and rises to become a holy temple in the Lord. And in him you too are being built together to become a dwelling in which God lives by his Spirit" (Ephesians 2:17-22).

Be a what God has made you! Be a living stone in the spiritual house of God's holy people.

Be What God Has Made You:
A Part of the Body of Christ!

The body is a unit, though it is made up of many parts; and though all its parts are many, they form one body. If the whole body were an eye, where would the sense of hearing be? If the whole body were an ear, where would the sense of smell be? But in fact God has arranged the parts in the body, every one of them, just as he wanted them to be. God has combined the members of the body so that there should be no division in the body, but that its parts should have equal concern for each other. If one part suffers, every part suffers with it; if one part is honored, every part rejoices with it. Now you are the body of Christ, and each one of you is a part of it. (1 Corinthians 12:12-27, selected verses)

Paul's picture of believers as the "body of Christ" is one of the most powerful and enduring word pictures in the New Testament. We are all parts of one body, and Christ is our Head. It's such a perfect metaphor that today the "body of Christ" has become a synonym for "The Church" (big C) — all believers everywhere.

When Paul used the picture of the "body of Christ" with the Corinthians, though, he had a very specific idea in mind. The Corinthian congregation had many problems, one of which was that some of its members had been blessed with amazing spiritual gifts. But instead of being a cause for rejoicing, these spiritual gifts became a source for grumbling (as members jealously coveted each others' gifts) and spiritual arrogance (as members with "better" gifts looked down on those with "lesser" gifts). To counter this strife and division, Paul used the picture of the unity-in-diversity that is found in the human body as a metaphor for the way believers relate to one another.

First and foremost, a body is *united*. It is a single unit that has an individual identity. "God has arranged the parts of the body so that there should be no division in the body," Paul writes. In the same way, the body of Christ is also united. In a sense, we subordinate our own needs, rights, and even identity for the good of the whole Church, the unity of believers. Paul writes elsewhere, "There is neither Jew nor Greek, slave nor free, male nor female, for you are all one in Christ Jesus" (Galatians 3:28). The spiritual arrogance that was ripping the congregation apart was wrong, because the body of Christ is a single, united, whole — "if one part is honored, every part rejoices with it."

But a body, though united, is also *diverse*. It is made of many parts which each perform a different, complementary job so that the body works. The whole body isn't an eye, or an ear, or a toe. In the same way, not all Christians have the same gifts. The grumbling, grass-is-always-greener mentality that causes some Christians to covet the gifts that God has seen fit to give to other Christians is really self-defeating. In Christ, we are united, yes — but we're not identical. Imagine if every teacher in a Christian school were a math teacher. Everyone would be the "equal," but the function of the school as a whole would be much more limited. The whole congregation can't be the pastor, or the treasurer, or the musicians. It is the diversity of individual gifts, working together, which corporately blesses the body of Christ.

But a body doesn't just work together, it's also broken together. A body with a broken toe doesn't say to itself, "Well, it's only a toe. I guess I'll just ignore it, and try to carry on as well as I can." No — "if one part suffers, every part suffers with it." The body as a whole has to work together so that it can be restored wholly to health.

The Church, like a body, is unity-in-diversity: "a unit... made up of many parts." A group of Christians is only as healthy as its weakest member. A congregation doesn't say to itself, "Well, we're doing OK, but the men in our congregation are all adulterers and drunks. I guess we should ignore the problem, and try to get along as well as we can." No — the church works together to gently correct and admonish the part that is weak, "speaking the truth in love" so that the entire congregation, as the body of Christ, will "in all things grow up into him who is the Head, that is, Christ" (Ephesians 4:15).

So, how does this all come about? How can we, individually and corporately, be the unity-in-diversity that is the body of Christ? Well, without getting too deep into sacramental theology, one way is the Lord's Supper. "Is not the bread that we break a participation in the body of Christ? Because there is one loaf, we, who are many, are one body, for we all partake of the one loaf" (1 Corinthians 10:16-17). Holy Communion is a sharing in the very body of Christ. By *taking* the body of Christ, we *become* the body of Christ. Or, as Father Alexander Schmemann states succinctly yet profoundly, "Man is what he eats."

The more we focus on Christ alone, the more he draws us closer to himself through Word and Sacrament, and the more we imitate him by daily acts of love and prayer, the closer we will naturally come to other members of his body, the Church, to be the unity-in-diversity of the body of Christ which God has made us.

Be What God Has Made You: A Branch of the True Vine!

I am the true vine, and my Father is the gardener. He cuts off every branch in me that bears no fruit, while every branch that does bear fruit he prunes so that it will be even more fruitful. You are already clean because of the word I have spoken to you. Remain in me, and I will remain in you. No branch can bear fruit by itself; it must remain in the vine. Neither can you bear fruit unless you remain in me.

I am the vine; you are the branches. If a man remains in me and I in him, he will bear much fruit; apart from me you can do nothing. If anyone does not remain in me, he is like a branch that is thrown away and withers; such branches are picked up, thrown into the fire and burned. If you remain in me and my words remain in you, ask whatever you wish, and it will be given you. This is to my Father's glory, that you bear much fruit, showing yourselves to be my disciples. (John 15:1-8)

This text takes us to Holy Thursday evening, the night that Jesus washed his disciple's feet in an upper room, instituted the Lord's Supper, and was betrayed by Judas Iscariot into the hands of his enemies. There was a lot on Jesus' mind that night, and he shared much of it with his disciples. One of the beautiful truths he taught them was the fact, "I am in my Father, and you are in me, and I am in you" (John 14:20). Like all good teachers, though, Jesus didn't count on his students learning this lesson the first time. So later that evening, he reiterated this important lesson by using a vivid picture to explain the relationship between the Father, the Son, and the followers.

God had used the image of his people as his vine several times in the Old Testament (Isaiah 5:1-8, Psalm 80:8-16), always as a sign of how he tended to them and took care of them. But God's people had turned against the Lord and become a "corrupt, wild vine" (Jeremiah 2:21). Therefore, Jesus came as the "true vine," who would fulfill God's purpose in the world. We, by God's grace, are branches of the true vine — connected to Jesus in faith. This is the beautiful picture of John 15.

Branches that are connected to the vine bear fruit. If a branch does not bear fruit, that is a sign that it is not connected to the branch, despite appearances to the contrary. Lack of fruit means that something is wrong with the connection; life-giving nourishment does not pass from the vine into the branch. The gardener's job is to find those unproductive branches and cut them off, throw them into the fire, and burn them. This very evening revealed one who appeared to be connected to Jesus and was not: Judas Iscariot, who had already left on his treacherous errand.

However, believers who remain in Jesus have the promise that he will remain in them, so that they bear much fruit. What is the fruit that Jesus promises? The Bible tells us, "the fruit of the Spirit is love, joy, peace, patience, kindness, goodness, faithfulness, gentleness and self-control" (Galatians 5:22-23). When we are connected to Christ and remain in him by faith, we will be branches that bear much fruit.

The Father also prunes fruitful branches so that they are even more productive. His pruning is the removal of what remains of our old, sinful nature as we grow in faith. This pruning may be unpleasant at first. It may come in the form of discipline, or even suffering. Think, for example, of the pruning that the disciples were about to face over the next 72 hours: the Father pruned away many of their old, selfish, misconceptions about who Jesus was and what he came to do. And yet, on the other side of this trial, they would be stronger and more fruitful vines.

A detail that we miss in English is the relation between "prune" in verse 2 and "clean" in verse 3. In Greek, these are the same word. The Father "prunes" us (cleans off the old, dead parts) and leaves us "clean" (pruned of our sinful nature; that is, forgiven and justified) through the word of forgiveness that Jesus speaks to us. When we remain in Jesus, and his words remain in us, we are cleansed from our sins and we bear much fruit. Theologically speaking, this cleansing of our sins is called "justification," and the life of fruit-bearing that follows is called "sanctification." We are forgiven of our sins and empowered to do good works through faith in Jesus Christ.

All of this, Jesus says, is "to my Father's glory." He tells his disciples, "let your light shine before men, that they may see your good deeds and praise your Father in heaven" (Matthew 5:16). The mark of discipleship is practicing the greatest of the fruits of faith: "By this all men will know that you are my disciples, if you *love one another*" (John 13:35). We are not saved because of the fruit that we bear. We bear fruit because we are saved. This fruit brings glory to God and benefit to our neighbor. As Luther said, "God doesn't need our good works, but our neighbor does." In our relationship with other Christians, let us be what God has made us: one of the branches of the True Vine, producing fruit for the glory of God and for the benefit of others.

Be What God Has Made You: A Royal Priest!

But you are a chosen people, a royal priesthood, a holy nation, a people belonging to God, that you may declare the praises of him who called you out of darkness into his wonderful light. (1 Peter 2:9)

As often as we have heard this passage, it may have slipped our notice that the phrase "royal priesthood," like some of the other phrases we have considered in this book (like "living sacrifice" and "free slave") is a jarring paradox, a surprising turn of phrase that would have caused Peter's first listeners to sit up and pay attention. In the context of the Old Testament, there's almost no such thing as a "royal priest." Priests were from the tribe of Levi, kings were supposed to come from Judah. Priests were priests and kings were kings, and rarely did anyone ever do both jobs.

So rarely, in fact, that there are only two instances in Scripture of someone who was both a king and a priest. The first was Melchizedek. This enigmatic figure appears for a brief scene in the book of Genesis with the Patriarch Abraham and then disappears. We know almost nothing about him, only that he was both "king of Salem" and a "priest of God most high" (Genesis 14:18). There is only one more mention of him in the Old Testament, a passing reference in Psalm 110. Then in the New Testament, the writer to the Hebrews describes Melchizedek with these words: "Without father or mother, without genealogy, without beginning of days or end of life, like the Son of God he remains a priest forever" (Hebrews 7:3).

Of course, the king-priest Melchizedek is a type, or picture, of the second, greatest King-Priest, Jesus Christ. The writer of Hebrews has this to say about Jesus:

> It is clear that our Lord descended from Judah, and in regard to that tribe Moses said nothing about priests. And what we have said is even more clear if another priest like Melchizedek appears, one who has become a priest not on the basis of a regulation as to his ancestry but on the basis of the power of an indestructible life… Because of this oath, Jesus has become the guarantee of a better covenant… Such a high priest meets our need — one who is holy, blameless, pure, set apart from sinners, exalted above the heavens. Unlike the other high priests, he does not need to offer sacrifices day after day, first for his own sins, and then for the sins of the people. He sacrificed for their sins once for all when he offered himself. For the law appoints as high priests men who are weak; but the oath, which came after the law, appointed the Son, who has been made perfect forever. (Hebrews 7:14-28)

And now, in this amazing text from Peter, we see that we are also kings and priests, royal priests of our Lord Jesus Christ. "You are a royal priesthood," Peter declares. In the Old Testament, the priest stood between God and the people, bringing the peoples' sacrifices and declaring the Lord's blessing, while a king, of course, stood in authority over the people. But now, because of the once-and-for-all work of our King-Priest Jesus Christ, we occupy the exalted position of both priest and king. As one Bible commentator puts it, "no one stands between us and God, and no one stands over us in our relation to God... [this phrase "royal priesthood" shows] the exaltation of our position and our function: the constant, direct, immediate contact with God." We are numbered with the saints in heaven, whom Jesus "made to be a kingdom and priests to serve our God, and they will reign on the earth" (Revelation 5:10).

Old Testament priests offered sacrifices to God on behalf of the people. Today, as God's New Testament priests, we offer "spiritual sacrifices acceptable to God through Jesus Christ" (1 Peter 2:5). As the ancient priests of Israel made sacrifices that pointed ahead to Jesus' ultimate sacrifice on the cross, we look back in faith at that same cross and, through Christ, make our own spiritual sacrifices to God.

What are those spiritual sacrifices? Allow me to mention a few: "a sacrifice of praise" (Hebrews 13:15); "do good and to share with others" (Hebrews 13:16); "offer your bodies as living sacrifices, holy and pleasing to God—this is your spiritual act of worship" (Romans 12:1); "The gifts you sent are a fragrant offering, an acceptable sacrifice" (Philippians 4:18); "live a life of love, just as Christ loved us and gave himself up for us as a fragrant offering and sacrifice to God" (Ephesians 5:2); and "to be a minister of Christ Jesus to the Gentiles with the priestly duty of proclaiming the gospel of God, so that the Gentiles might become an offering acceptable to God, sanctified by the Holy Spirit" (Romans 15:16).

Many people today think that Christianity is mainly concerned with what comes *after* death — how to "get right with God" in order to avoid hell and get to heaven. But as we see the identity that God has given us as royal priests, we see that Christianity is just as concerned with what comes *before* death — how to use the time he has given us in service to others as kings and priests.

Father Lawrence Farley writes, "God calls us, as His royal priesthood, to deliver ourselves and our world into His hands, for He is the helper of the helpless, the hope of the hopeless, the savior of the storm-tossed, the haven of the voyager, the physician of the sick." Be what God has made you! Be a royal priest!

✠

Be What God Has Made You: Devoted to Prayer!

Devote yourselves to prayer, being watchful and thankful. (Colossians 4:2)

How many sermons, chapels, devotions, and Bible classes have you ever heard on the topic of prayer? My guess is, if you've been a Christian for longer than about ten minutes, you've heard quite a lot about prayer in your life. It's a justifiably popular topic among preachers, teachers, and writers of devotional material. After all, it's one of the most basic, even essential, parts of being a Christian. I'm guessing that most of the people reading this devotion could give a very effective personal testimony to the power of prayer. Most of us know the "talking points" — the Adoration, Confession, Thanksgiving, and Supplication (ACTS) acronym (or something like it), the model prayer that our Savior taught us to pray (only one-seventh of which is for physical or material things!), and Paul's oft-quoted encouragement to "pray continually" (1 Thessalonians 5:17). I'm even betting that most of the readers of this devotion are better "pray-ers" than I am, and so it is hard write about a topic so dear to all of us as prayer.

And yet, as we continue our look into what God has made us in regard to our life together as believers in this world, it is important to take a look at the topic of prayer. As Christians, individually and collectively, we are — and we are to be — devoted to prayer. The word translated "devoted" here in Colossians (also in Acts 2:42) has the meaning of "to be busily engaged in; to hold fast to, to continue or persevere in." One non-biblical Greek source uses this word in conjunction with a siege — the besieger has to be constantly engaged in the siege, and hold fast and persevere, in order for the siege to succeed. So it is with our prayer (see Luke 18:1-6).

One of the greatest Scriptural examples of a bold, persistent prayer is that of Abraham, pleading with God about the promised destruction of the city of Sodom. Abraham begs God to spare the city and asks, "What if there are fifty righteous people in the city? Will you really sweep it away and not spare the place for the sake of the fifty righteous people in it? Far be it from you to do such a thing — to kill the righteous with the wicked, treating the righteous and the wicked alike. Far be it from you! Will not the Judge of all the earth do right?" (Genesis 18:24-25).

Much could be said about Abraham's prayer, especially about the boldness of his subsequent prayers as he finally gets God to agree to spare the city for the sake of only ten righteous people. Much could also be said about God — a God who, though sovereign, deigns to listen to our prayers and take them into consideration as he governs the world; a God who, though perfectly just, condescends to show mercy in not destroying the wicked for the sake of the righteous; a God who, though perfectly loving, still burns with righteous anger over sinners and their sin; a God who, in spite of not finding even ten righteous people in Sodom, still answers Abraham's prayer and rescues Lot and his family from the promised destruction.

Much could indeed be said about these things, but allow me to turn the tables for a second. Imagine our President pleading with God for the United States of America. God promises destruction on account of our sinfulness, and the President pleads for mercy on behalf of the righteous people that God might find here. How far would the President have to go? Could fifty righteous be found? Twenty? Ten? One? How many righteous people are there in the United States?

We know that on the basis of our own merit, our own works, our own good intentions, our own "devotion" to prayer, that we fall far short of the righteous standard God requires of us. We know that in spite of the President's best efforts on our behalf, we would fall under the same curse as the city of Sodom. But thanks be to God that he does not judge us on our own merit, but instead looks at us and sees Christ. Thanks be to God that we are not saved because of our prayers, but because of our Savior — "In him we might become the righteousness of God" (2 Corinthians 5:21). Thanks be to God that, as we trust in him who justifies the wicked, our "faith is credited as righteousness" (Romans 4:5). Thanks be to God, that through Jesus' atoning blood we have access to the Most Holy Place (see Hebrews 10:19) — that we will bodily stand in God's living presence someday, and that until then, we have the high privilege to come spiritually before God's throne in prayer. We are all righteous by faith in Jesus.

God has given us the wonderful blessing of prayer. Let us be diligent in the use of this gift, for ourselves, our families, our fellow Christians, our enemies, and the world. Let us follow the advice of St. James, and listen to his stirring promise: "Therefore confess your sins to each other and pray for each other so that you may be healed. The prayer of a righteous man is powerful and effective" (James 5:16).

✠

Be What God Has Made You: A Minister of Reconciliation!

All this is from God, who reconciled us to himself through Christ and gave us the ministry of reconciliation: that God was reconciling the world to himself in Christ, not counting men's sins against them. And he has committed to us the message of reconciliation. (2 Corinthians 5:18-19)

In an earlier devotion, we considered the fact that God has made us *reconciled*. Looking at Colossians 1:21-22, we saw that we had been alienated from God by our evil behavior, but that God, through Christ's death, ended our alienation and brought us back to himself so that we would be holy in his sight. Now we are taking that reconciliation one step further: having been reconciled, we now receive a *ministry* of reconciliation.

Our verse begins with the words "all this." *All this* — this blessing of reconciliation — is from God. God bridged the gap that existed between his holiness and sinful humanity through Christ, and all this is a gift of his divine grace. As Paul reminds us, "It is by grace you have been saved, through faith — and this not from yourselves, it is the gift of God — not by works, so that no one can boast" (Ephesians 2:8-9). We did nothing to reconcile ourselves; it is God who does everything to save us.

Having done everything to save us, though, God does something surprising: He turned things over to us. After completing his work on the cross and rising from the dead, Jesus ascended into heaven and left his followers to carry on his work.

Paul writes, "He has committed *to us* the message of reconciliation." As we considered in our devotion on "Jars of Clay," God does not do the work of preaching and teaching his Word directly from heaven. He uses intermediaries — ministers. He uses *us*.

"Us." The question can be asked: who is meant by that word? Is it Paul and Timothy, the two men listed as the writers of Second Corinthians? Is it all of the apostles? Is it some priestly caste of bishops and presbyters who rule the church by divine fiat? Just who, exactly, are the ministers of reconciliation? Look closely at the word "us" and see all the places it appears in these two verses. God "reconciled *us*... and gave *us* the ministry of reconciliation... and he has committed to *us* the message of reconciliation." It couldn't be more plain — *all* who are reconciled are made ministers of reconciliation. Every Christian believer is a minister of reconciliation.

What is a minister? A minister is a servant, a helper. A minister is also someone who holds a specific office or position, not to "lord it over" others, but, again, to serve them and put their needs above his or her own, just as Jesus himself "did not come to be served, but to serve, and to give his life as a ransom for many" (Matthew 20:28).

Look closely at these verses, and notice that there are no conditions attached to the message of reconciliation. There is no "if... then." Jesus' work on the cross, although it was done for us, did not involve us in any way, nor does it need any sort of action or assent on our part to become true. In this way, it is *objective* — that is, relating to actual historical facts, and not merely our internal subjective beliefs or perceptions. Professor David Valleskey writes:

> A right understanding of the objective fact of a God-effected universal reconciliation in Christ is important also for [us]. Our message is not, "If you believe, God will no longer charge your sins against you." It is, "In Christ, what needs to be done has been done. God no longer charges your sins against you. Believe."

God counted Jesus' death as the full payment for every sin ever committed. Christ really died on a real cross, to really reconcile the world to himself — whether we believe it or not. The fact that some people won't believe, and reject the message we bring them (and therefore do not receive the benefits of it) does not change the fact that *it is true*.

This fact makes our job as ministers clear. We are simply to announce the glorious message that God has reconciled the world to himself in Christ, and trust that God will change hearts through that message. And we can be sure that he is still reconciling the world today, as the Holy Spirit brings more and more people into personal possession of saving faith and effects individual, subjective reconciliation by means of the "message of reconciliation" that we preach.

As reconciled ministers, we have received from God "the message of reconciliation" with which we are to serve others. It's that simple. What we have, we are to pass on, in the same spirit as Paul, who wrote, "For I received from the Lord what I also passed on to you" (1 Corinthians 11:23). The *New Living Translation* makes this apparent when it translates the last part of verse 19: "This is the wonderful message he has given us to tell others." May we always do so, for Jesus' sake.

Be What God Has Made You: Your Brother's Keeper!

Then the Lord said to Cain, "Where is your brother Abel?"

"I don't know," he replied. "Am I my brother's keeper?" (Genesis 4:9)

We've all heard it before. Whether from the mouths of our children, someone else's teenager, or even in rebellious, petulant words coming from our own mouths, we've all heard questions like Cain's. "What?" the question goes, with a sarcastic turn of the upper lip, "Do you *really* expect me to _____?" It's almost a challenge, as the questioner fills in the blank with an action that (to him at least) seems completely unreasonable. "Do you *really* expect me to be my brother's keeper?"

Over centuries of Bible commentaries, Cain has taken a lot of criticism for this question, and rightly so. After all, he knows exactly where his brother is: lying dead in a field, killed by Cain's own hand in what was apparently a premeditated murder inspired by pouty, jealous rivalry. But if you, like me, are an oldest child, weren't there times in your life when you were sick of keeping track of your younger siblings' whereabouts and being held accountable for their actions? Isn't it a little unreasonable of God to expect Cain to be his brother's "keeper"?

The word Cain uses for "keeper" is from one of my favorite Hebrew verbs, *shamar*. This verb can mean "take care of" or "guard," and is used to describe the providential care God has for us. One can also *shamar* things like houses, cities, children, or flocks. And so Cain asks, with the righteous indignation of a put-upon older brother, "Am I my brother's keeper? Do you *really* expect me to watch over my brother the same way he watches over those stupid sheep?" It has even been said that Cain was, in effect, telling God, "I'm not my brother's keeper — that's *your* job!"

Well, what is the answer to Cain's question? Is he his brother's keeper, or not? Cain doesn't seem to think so. In his conversation with Cain, God doesn't answer the question directly either. But the rest of Scripture is perfectly clear on the matter: Yes. We are our brother's keeper. Actually, that should be brothers' and sisters' — plural and inclusive. One of our greatest jobs as Christians is to look out for one another.

We are to take care of one another physically. Paul reminds us, "As we have opportunity, let us do good to all people, especially to those who belong to the family of believers" (Galatians 6:10). John asks rhetorically, "If anyone has material possessions and sees his brother in need but has no pity on him, how can the love of God be in him?" (1 John 3:17). James praises religion that "look[s] after orphans and widows in their distress" (James 1:27). Ancient Christians risked their lives taking care of brothers and sisters who were in prison for their faith; by visiting the martyrs, even burying their animal-torn bodies, many of them became martyrs too.

We also are to look after one another spiritually. Again, Paul writes, "Brothers, if someone is caught in a sin, you who are spiritual should restore him gently" (Galatians 6:1). John encourages us, "If anyone sees his brother commit a sin that does not lead to death, he should pray and God will give him life" (1 John 5:15). The prophet Ezekiel was made "watchman for the house of Israel" (Ezekiel 33:7), and it was his explicit duty to warn his people of the spiritual danger they were in because of their sin.

Above all, Jesus summarizes: "Love your neighbor as yourself" (Mark 12:31). Romans 13:10 says, "love is the fulfillment of the law." Love isn't just emotions and feelings. Love is deeds and actions. When John tells us that "God is love" (1 John 4:8), he isn't so much telling us who God is or how God feels, but about *what God does*.

God doesn't just sit up in heaven, watching us like a permissive and doting grandfather, fawning over everything good we do and looking the other way at our sins. No. God's love is love in motion, that springs into action and rescues us who are the objects of his love, in spite of our desires to the contrary. Twice in his first epistle John tells us "this is what love is" and then names an *action* (3:16 and 4:9). Both of those passages tell us what

God did for us: he sent his Son who laid down his life. God doesn't just tell us how he feels about us. God shows his love by what he does for us, "that while we were still sinners, Christ died for us" (Romans 5:8).

In the same way, our love for our brothers and sisters in Christ is characterized by an active caring for them, physically and spiritually. Cook for them. Pray for them. Hug them. Rebuke them. Praise them. Critique them. Love them, as God loves you in Christ. As John says, "Do not be like Cain… We should love one another" (1 John 3:11-12).

The Apostle Paul writes in 2 Corinthians 4:13 (quoting Psalm 116), "I believed; therefore I have spoken." Believing certain things causes us to act in certain ways. Our faith in Jesus Christ as our Savior makes us act in a new and loving way towards others.

Are you your brother's keeper? Yes! — because that is what God has made you.

✠

Part Four:
Your Relationship to the World

Be What God Has Made You:
An Alien and a Stranger!

Dear friends, I urge you, as aliens and strangers in the world, to abstain from sinful desires, which war against your soul. (1 Peter 2:11)

This devotion begins the fourth section of our theme. In this final section, we will be considering our role and place "in the world" (to use Peter's own words), as we are encouraged to be what God has made us in relation to the world at large.

The idea of being an "alien and a stranger" is not one that began with Peter. The Patriarch Abraham called himself an "alien and a stranger" among the Hittite people (Genesis 23:4) as he tried to acquire a place to bury his wife Sarah. Although someday all of Canaan would belong to Abraham's family as a promised inheritance (Genesis 12:7), at that time he did not own any land at all, not even a place to bury his dead. He was an "alien and a stranger." He sojourned among the Hittites, but he was not one of them. He was an outsider who had neither claim on the land nor the rights of a citizen.

The writer to the Hebrews speaks of Abraham and the other early patriarchs:

An Alien and a Stranger!

> All these people were still living by faith when they died. They did not receive the things promised; they only saw them and welcomed them from a distance. And they admitted that they were aliens and strangers on earth. People who say such things show that they are looking for a country of their own. If they had been thinking of the country they had left, they would have had opportunity to return. Instead, they were longing for a better country — a heavenly one. (Hebrews 11:13-16)

Abraham left his birthplace at God's command. He heard the mighty promises of God in his lifetime. But he did not live to see them all fulfilled. He lived by faith in things unseen. He considered himself an "alien and a stranger." He did not think about his old homeland, nor did he sink deep roots in his new country. When he died, the only land he owned was the cave in which he and his wife were buried. He was not a resident of any country on this earth. He was not a resident of this earth at all. Instead, he was a citizen of "a better country — a heavenly one" (Hebrews 11:16).

We are all citizens of this country and residents of our state. Many of us own land and houses and property. We carry drivers' licenses and passports. We pay taxes and vote. But we are still aliens and strangers in this world. Notice here that Peter doesn't say "act like aliens and strangers and abstain from sinful desires." He says, "*As* aliens and strangers in the world, abstain from sinful desires." He isn't giving a command as much as he is stating a fact. God has called us out of this world and made us aliens here and citizens of heaven. So Peter says, in effect, "You *are* aliens. Be what you God has made you."

How are we to be aliens? Paul has this advice: "Do not conform any longer to the pattern of this world, but be transformed by the renewing of your mind" (Romans 12:2). A right relationship to God changes our relationship to the world. We don't buy in to this world's standards of value. We don't set our hearts on "earthly things" (Colossians 3:2). Instead, we renew our minds, letting the transforming power of God change and re-make our attitudes. "Abstain from sinful *desires*," says Peter — which is often quite a bit harder than abstaining from sinful actions!

Then Peter suggests that we let our conduct set us apart: "Live such good lives among the pagans that, though they accuse you of doing wrong, they may see your good deeds and glorify God on the day he visits us" (1 Peter 2:12). We don't follow a worldly pattern of behavior. We don't do the things "they" do. Jesus says, "In the same way, let your light shine before men, that they may see your good deeds and praise your Father in heaven" (Matthew 5:16). We are aliens and strangers. We are different.

I've been to a lot of foreign countries, most of them Spanish-speaking. In spite of my experience in travel, my knowledge of the culture and customs, and my decent command of the language, I have never once been mistaken for a native. Why not? *Because I'm a foreigner*. I look different. I act differently. I talk differently. I do different things. But how many times have I, by blending in with the world, been mistaken for a citizen of this world? All too many, I'm sure.

Is this true for you, too? Do you conform too much to the "pattern of this world"? Do you pursue earthly things and declare your allegiance to something other than, and therefore less than, God? Are you not-so-alien and not-so-strange anymore? If so, join me on my knees, confessing my sin before God, the Father of our Lord Jesus Christ, the King of heaven where our real citizenship lies. Join me in thankful remembrance that sins are forgiven for Jesus' sake, and then join me in living my life *in* this world, but not as part *of* this world. Join me in being an alien and a stranger, just as God has made us.

Be What God Has Made You: Salt and Light!

You are the salt of the earth... You are the light of the world. (Matthew 5:13-14)

This verse comes from Jesus' Sermon on the Mount. The words of this sermon are some of the most famous in all of Scripture, and are often quoted (and misquoted!) by Christians and non-Christians alike. When studying this sermon, it's important to remember that Jesus preached it to *believers* — to "his disciples" (Matthew 5:1) who recognized him as the Lord's promised Messiah. Without that fact in mind, some of Jesus' words become impossible to understand correctly.

"You are the salt of the earth." "You are the light of the world." To an unbeliever, these words mean nothing. But to believers, they are words of comfort, promise, and encouragement. Let's explore what it means that God has made us salt and light.

First, believers are called "salt." In ancient times, salt was used primarily as a preservative to keep food from spoiling. In the same way, Christians are a blessing to the world, preserving it from a total slide into moral chaos by living quiet lives of common decency and teaching our children to do the same. Witness the dramatic evils of Sodom and Gomorrah, where not even ten righteous people could be found, or the wretched state of the world before the Flood, when Noah alone was righteous in his generation (see Genesis 7:1). God would have saved Sodom and Gomorrah if there had been enough righteous people there; by God's grace, Noah and his family literally *were* the world that God saved (see 1 Peter 3:20). Unfortunately, however, the preserving qualities of Christians in the world are usually most conspicuous by their absence.

But far more importantly, Christians bless and preserve the world by blessing the Lord, and by preserving and teaching his Word to those around us. We are called to teach God's Word to our children (Deuteronomy 11:19). We are told to be ready to give an account to anyone — especially an unbeliever — who asks us "to give the reason for the hope that [we] have" (1 Peter 3:15). All of our words are to be "seasoned with salt," so that they are "full of grace" to those who listen (Colossians 4:6). We are to do all of these things, witnessing to Christ in our words and actions, because "salvation is found in no one else, for there is no other name under heaven given to men by which we must be saved" (Acts 4:12). For "how can they believe in the one of whom they have not heard?" (Romans 10:14). Christ saves and preserves this world through us.

How is this mighty thing possible? How is it possible that our puny words and our misguided actions could be used to preserve this earth as salt preserves food? The answer is simple and amazing: Christ and his kingdom dwell in us (Luke 17:21), changing not only us, but also, through us, changing and blessing the whole earth.

The world, however, would prefer if we were sugar instead of salt. With cleansing there is sometimes a sting, and the world would rather be pardoned than purified. Many teachers "de-salt" their teaching, and thus desalinate their followers. In the same way, many in the world are more than happy to live in darkness. Jesus himself said, "This is the verdict: Light has come into the world, but men loved darkness instead of light because their deeds were evil" (John 3:19).

Christians, though, are "the light of the world." We live on Mount Zion, "the city of the great King" (Psalm 48:2). In a world of darkness, the Church, the great communion of saints, is a safe place in the darkness, with light and food and walls and friends, a city on a hill that "cannot be hidden" (Matthew 5:14), which the "gates of Hades will not overcome" (Matthew 16:18).

What do we, as the light of the world, illuminate? Christ. We are like the spotlights in a museum, highlighting a masterpiece for all to see. Jesus' light shines on us, and we reflect it back. When we do, as we shine our light on Jesus, those in the sin-darkened world "see [our] good deeds and praise [our] Father in heaven" (Matthew 5:16).

Finally, take careful note of the verb used in this verse. "Are" states a fact. Many preachers make this an admonition, "should be," and wield these verses as a club. But it is so much stronger to state the fact and let the Holy Spirit do his work in our hearts. We believers *are* salt. We *are* light. Our faith in Jesus makes us so. Just going about our humdrum, workaday lives brings salt and light to the world around us.

Here again, in the Sermon on the Mount, Jesus is saying, "Be what God has made you." You are salt. You are light. Be salty! Shine! Not just by doing "good deeds" or being a "nice person," but by living your faith to preserve the world, and by shining your light in a way that will illuminate Jesus and give glory to the Father in heaven.

Be What God Has Made You: Hated!

If the world hates you, keep in mind that it hated me first. If you belonged to the world, it would love you as its own. As it is, you do not belong to the world, but I have chosen you out of the world. That is why the world hates you. Remember the words I spoke to you: "No servant is greater than his master." If they persecuted me, they will persecute you also. (John 15:18-20)

Wow. This is a tough one. Don't we all generally want to be popular, or at least liked? It would be one thing if the world simply ignored us and let us be. But it doesn't, and Jesus promised that it won't. The world will hate us for being Christians. We know not to put too much stock into the world's opinion of us. We know not to go out of our way to ingratiate ourselves to the me-first world or buy into its culture of death, but it still stings when we see just how brutally the world hates us. And hate us it does.

On the one hand, yes. We do try to be "liked." It's important to put as few barriers in the way of the Gospel as possible. It's important not to go out of our way to be obnoxious or sectarian or standoffish. Like Paul, we should "become all things to all men" (1 Corinthians 9:22) so that we can reach as many as possible with the Gospel message. But we ultimately need to remember that the ways of God are not the ways of man (see Isaiah 55:8). If we compete to earn the unconditional love and acceptance of the world, we will end up conforming ourselves to a set of standards that is not God's.

And so, as we live our lives as Christians, we need to remember that the world *will* hate us. If we belonged to the world, we would be accepted by the world. But we belong to God — and as the world rejected Christ, it will surely reject us as well. Jesus said, "I have given them your word and the world has hated them, for they are not of the world any more than I am of the world" (John 17:14).

If it seems unpleasant to be rejected and hated by the world, let's consider the alternative: being rejected and hated by God. It's a situation we know well, for we were all at one time friends of the world and enemies of God. The simple truth is that before we became believers by the power of the Holy Spirit, God hated us.

In fact, is entirely consistent with Biblical revelation to say that *God hates sinners*. Not just sin; God in the glory of his justice hates all sinners. And without Christ, God would still hate us as the wretched sinners that we are. Yes, he loves me (John 3:16) — but I dare not minimize the depth of my depravity, which held me guilty as a sinner before God "from the time my mother conceived me" (Psalm 51:5). Consider Psalm 5:5, which says, "The arrogant cannot stand in your presence; you hate all who do wrong." (Also see Leviticus 20:23; Deuteronomy 32:40-42; Psalm 11:5; Proverbs 6:16-19; Isaiah 63:10; Jeremiah 12:7-8; and Hosea 9:15.)

We were by nature God's enemies and objects of his wrath. He hated us. But he also loved us. We've discussed some paradoxes in this book, but the greatest paradox in history is that the God who hates sinners also loves them, and sent his one and only Son to save them. Without seeing anything good in us, without waiting for any merit or action or choice or decision on our part, entirely because of his grace and mercy, and while we were still sinners, Christ died for us. Paul concludes: "Since we have now been justified by his blood, how much more shall we be saved from God's wrath through him! For if, when we were God's enemies, we were reconciled to him through the death of his Son, how much more, having been reconciled, shall we be saved through his life!" (Romans 5:9-10).

Thanks be to God! Through Christ, he has destroyed our alliance with this world and its prince (more on that in the next section) and restored our relationship with himself. God no longer hates us — in Christ, he loves us completely. Our newfound alliance with God seriously affects our relationship to the world, to the extent that we "will be hated by all nations because of [Jesus]" (Matthew 24:9). Compared to the love of God, however, it is only a small matter that we have lost the love of the world. Paul writes "I consider everything a loss compared to the surpassing greatness of knowing Christ Jesus my Lord, for whose sake I have lost all things. I consider them rubbish, that I may gain Christ and be found in him" (Philippians 3:8).

The hatred of the world is rubbish, but it should come as no surprise. "Do not be surprised, my brothers, if the world hates you" (1 John 3:13). What do we do with this hatred from the world? First, let us rejoice that we are counted worthy to suffer disgrace for the Name (see Acts 5:41). Second, let us remember Jesus' words from Matthew 5:44, "Love your enemies and pray for those who persecute you." And finally, let us reflect on his awesome encouragement: "In this world you will have trouble. But take heart! I have overcome the world" (John 16:33).

Be What God Has Made You:
An Enemy of the Prince of This World!

And I will put enmity between you and the woman, and between your offspring and hers; he will crush your head, and you will strike his heel. (Genesis 3:15)

Can you imagine intentionally choosing to be the enemy of your best friend? That's essentially what Adam and Eve did during the sad episode we refer to as the Fall. Created in the "image and likeness" of their Holy Creator God (Genesis 1:26), with an intimate acquaintance and direct access to him that we can only imagine, the first humans were the certainly God's friends. But then, in a moment of weakness, temptation, deception, and doubt, they caved in to their misguided desires to be "like God" (Genesis 3:4) and broke the only commandment God had for them. They freely chose to become the enemy of their dearest friend, and instead became close friends with their mortal enemy.

The full effects of the Fall are too much to go into here, but one of its saddest effects is this tragic change of allegiance. Adam and Eve's sinful choice created *amity*, or friendship, between Satan and mankind. As the evil angels had fallen and become enemies of God (2 Peter 2:4; Jude 6), Adam and Eve had also defected from God and given their allegiance to Satan. So, the first Gospel proclamation after the Fall was God's announcement of his plan to (re)create *enmity*, or hatred, between Satan and the offspring of the woman as part of his plan to undo that cosmic betrayal.

Every human being was affected by the consequences of the Fall. "Sin entered the world through one man, and death through sin, and in this way death came to all men, because all sinned" (Romans 5:12). Sin made us enemies of the Lord and allies of Satan and his minions in their war against God. "The sinful mind is hostile to God" (Romans 8:7). Without Christ, we were caught on the wrong side of a losing battle — until, at last, God fulfilled that first promise of a Savior.

When Christ died on Calvary's cross, he broke the alliance between us and Satan and restored the primal hatred that properly belonged between the devil and the human race. When he rose victoriously on Easter morning, he destroyed the power of the grave and destroyed death, the "last enemy" (1 Corinthians 15:26). It's ironic that a promise of hatred (between us and Satan) is a promise of peace (between us and God), but that is what this *protevangel*, this first Gospel promise, is.

What does all of this mean for us now? It means that God has made us enemies of the prince of this world. It means that we are in a spiritual battle. It means that "our struggle is not against flesh and blood, but against the rulers, against the authorities, against the powers of this dark world and against the spiritual forces of evil in the heavenly realms" (Ephesians 6:12). It means that we have our work cut out for us.

For we are not fighting a weak enemy. Peter reminds us, "Your enemy the devil prowls around like a roaring lion looking for someone to devour" (1 Peter 5:8). John sees Satan as a "great dragon" and an "ancient serpent... who leads the whole world astray" (Revelation 12:9). He "masquerades as an angel of light" (2 Corinthians 11:14). He performs "counterfeit miracles, signs, and wonders" (2 Thessalonians 2:9). He is the "father of lies" (John 8:44) who can even "take away the word from [people's] hearts, so that they may not believe and be saved" (Luke 8:12). He is the one who afflicted Job, caused Peter to stumble, and convinced Judas Iscariot to betray his Savior.

But, as C. S. Lewis reminds us, there are two equal and opposite errors we can have concerning the devils: "One is to disbelieve in their existence. The other is to believe, and to feel an excessive and unhealthy interest in them." Yes, Satan is a terrible and powerful enemy. Yes, we must always be on our guard against him. But what was true about him 2,000 years ago is just as true today: "The prince of this world now stands condemned" (John 16:11). The devil is already beaten. Christ is the Victor. He has won the fight and vanquished our worst enemy. In our daily lives as Christians in the Church Militant, we continue the fight against this vanquished foe with the weapons that God has given us: the Name of Jesus (Acts 16:18), prayer [and fasting] (Mark 9:29), with the Word of God (Hebrews 4:12), and by the mighty panoply that God gives us:

> Therefore put on the full armor of God… the belt of truth buckled around your waist, with the breastplate of righteousness in place, and with your feet fitted with the readiness that comes from the gospel of peace. In addition to all this, take up the shield of faith, with which you can extinguish all the flaming arrows of the evil one. Take the helmet of salvation and the sword of the Spirit, which is the word of God. (Ephesians 6:13-17)

Our first parents made an enemy out of their dearest friend. God restored that friendship with a plan of salvation so amazing that we cannot fully comprehend it this side of heaven. In making us his friends, God also made us enemies of the prince of this world. Are we concerned? We should be. But the last word belongs to our God. Listen to these words from the Apostle John, directed to believers who, like us, were fighting against spiritual enemies: "You, dear children, are from God and have overcome them, because the one who is in you is greater than the one who is in the world" (1 John 4:4).

✠

Be What God Has Made You: His Ambassador!

We are therefore Christ's ambassadors, as though God were making his appeal through us. (2 Corinthians 5:20)

One of the many important jobs of the President of the United States is to appoint ambassadors to foreign nations. Sometimes, these ambassadorships are simply a way that a President can reward his friends and supporters with a prestigious position. At other times, though, the choice of ambassador to a critical nation with a delicate relationship to the US is an important decision, and the individual appointed could be the difference between success and failure, peace and war, life and death.

Whatever the circumstances of the appointment, though, ambassadors serve an important function. They personally represent their country to other nations. The person of the ambassador is afforded the same respect as the President himself. His embassy is considered US soil. The ambassador's words are his President's words. His promises carry the full faith and confidence of the nation he represents, and his threats do the same. To mistreat him is to insult his entire country; to eject him is to formally (and rudely) sever ties with the government who sent him.

It is an incredible privilege, then, that we are considered "Christ's ambassadors." We personally represent Christ and his kingdom to the world in which we live. Like a political ambassador, we do not speak our own words, but those of our sovereign: God makes his appeal "through us." The message of the Gospel that we bring does not rely on our authority, but on God's. We are "*Christ's* ambassadors," speaking "on *Christ's* behalf." As he sent out the 72 disciples, Jesus told them, "He who listens to you listens to me; he who rejects you rejects me" (Luke 10:16). He says the same to us.

As Christ's ambassadors, we plea to this world: "We implore you on Christ's behalf: Be reconciled to God" (2 Corinthians 5:20). As God's spokespeople, we make the offer of reconciliation, a peace treaty, between our holy king and sinful mankind.

The verse after our text gives the basis for this peace, "God made him who had no sin to be sin for us, so that in him we might become the righteousness of God" (2 Corinthians 5:21). Christ, who sent us into the world, came into this world himself to be our substitute. The sin of the world, our sin, was laid on his sinless shoulders. He was punished so that we might go free. He was cursed, and we have become the righteousness of God.

Now Jesus has returned to heaven to rule and reign, and we have been sent into the world to speak for him. Our job as ambassadors is to bring the message of God's mighty work, of forgiveness of sins through Christ, to the world in which we live.

An order of service that my church uses contains a public confession of sins followed by an announcement of forgiveness by the pastor. The words of the absolution say, in part, "I... announce the grace of God unto all of you, and in the stead and by the command of my Lord Jesus Christ, I forgive you all your sins, in the name of the Father and of the Son and of the Holy Ghost." Visitors are often shocked — how can that man say "I forgive you"? Isn't that God's job?

Yes, it is God's job. Therefore, it is also the job of God's ambassadors. Jesus gave us the authority to forgive sins when we became his disciples by faith, and he gives us the authority to speak "in his stead" as his ambassadors. "Jesus said, 'Peace be with you! As the Father has sent me, I am sending you.' And with that he breathed on them and said, 'Receive the Holy Spirit. If you forgive anyone his sins, they are forgiven; if you do not forgive them, they are not forgiven'"(John 20:21-23). What a mighty commissioning we have received from God!

One other job that ambassadors have is to carry messages or requests back to their homeland on behalf of the country to which they are sent. In the same way we, as Christ's ambassadors in this world, have the high privilege of interceding on behalf of this world in prayer. We do so in the words of the Lord's Prayer, "your will be done on earth as it is in heaven" (Matthew 6:10). We do so any time we lift up this fallen world, or one of its inhabitants, in "prayer... like incense" (Psalm 142:2) before God's throne in heaven (see also Revelation 8:3-4).

Announce God's good news to the world around you. Tell of his love, forgiveness, mercy, and grace. Speak and act with all the confidence and authority of Jesus himself. Intercede for the world, bringing its needs before God in prayer. Be an ambassador of Christ. Be what God has made you.

Be What God Has Made You:
Rescued From the Dominion of Darkness!

He has rescued us from the dominion of darkness and brought us into the kingdom of the Son he loves. (Colossians 1:13)

The word translated "rescued" in this dynamic passage of Scripture is synonymous with one of the most common Biblical metaphors of all — a metaphor so common that we don't even think of it as metaphorical anymore. "To be saved" (and all the expressions derived from it) is such a normal, everyday expression that it has come to be interchangeable with "to be a Christian," and overuse seems to have taken most of the original "oomph" out of this powerful and dramatic Scriptural word-picture.

"Saved" or "salvation" words in the Bible carry with them a connotation that is easier seen in words like "rescue" and "deliverance." The picture is snatching someone out of danger. Theologian J. A. O. Preus writes, "To 'save' a person is to rescue him or her from threatening circumstances and potential destruction." We see "saved" as a static thing: like money in a bank, we are set aside by God so we can go to heaven. But in the language of Scripture, being "saved" or having "salvation" is vigorous, lively, forceful, and exciting: a person hauled half-dead out of a swollen river, or pulled unconscious from a burning car, or rescued at the eleventh hour by commandos from a hostage situation gone bad.

We see this vivid drama of salvation and heroic rescue spread all across the pages of the Bible. The physical deliverance of the Children of Israel from slavery in Egypt is a foreshadowing of the spiritual deliverance that God has effected for his people through Jesus, his Son, who was also "called out of Egypt" (Matthew 2:15). Eight people were "saved though water" in Noah's ark, and "this water symbolizes baptism that now saves you also… by the resurrection of Jesus Christ, who has gone into heaven and is at God's right hand" (1 Peter 3:20-22). This salvation is both present and future. Jesus Christ "gave himself for our sins to rescue us from the *present* evil age" (Galatians 1:4), and he also "rescues us from the *coming* wrath" (1 Thessalonians 1:10).

God's salvation isn't a passive thing. It is a work of his power: "The LORD will lay bare his holy arm in the sight of all the nations, and all the ends of the earth will see the salvation of our God" (Isaiah 52:10). The Psalmist writes, "Sing to the LORD a new song, for he has done marvelous things; his right hand and his holy arm have worked salvation for him" (Psalm 98:1).

That salvation was indeed a powerful and active work of God, despite appearances to the contrary. As Dr. Preus further comments, "the 'mighty arm of God' was nailed, weak and dying, to the cross." But even in weakness, God's power is "made perfect" (2 Corinthians 12:9) — and that power of God is "for the salvation of everyone who believes" (Romans 1:16).

In the same way, this passage from Colossians pictures God as an active rescuer, swooping down to snatch us out of the danger in which we find ourselves. We were enmeshed in the "dominion of darkness" — not by an accident of birth, or a careless slip, or an honest mistake. We were part of that dominion of darkness, held in thrall to the Prince of Darkness as a result of our many intentional transgressions, our deliberate conscious choices, and our thoroughly corrupt sinful nature.

God our Savior, though, is more powerful than the forces holding us prisoner. The Lord is stronger than the dominion of darkness. Through Christ's work, he has defeated the devil, forgiven our sins, and delivered us from sin's power. We have been turned "from darkness to light" and "from the power of Satan to God" so that we "may receive forgiveness of sins and a place among those who are sanctified by faith" (Acts 26:18). We are no longer hostages and henchmen in the kingdom of darkness. We are sons and servants in the glorious kingdom of the Son.

We know Christ's kingdom is "not of this world" (John 18:36). But Christ's kingdom is not only heaven, waiting for us as a future reward. Christ's kingdom is *now*, wherever the power of the gospel rules in people's hearts and lives. "The kingdom of God is not a matter of eating and drinking, but of righteousness, peace and joy in the Holy Spirit" (Romans 14:17). When we pray "thy kingdom come" (Matthew 6:10), says Martin Luther, we are praying that "our heavenly Father give his Holy Spirit, so that by his grace we believe his holy Word and lead a godly life now on earth and forever in heaven."

Early Christians certainly understood the idea of God as our "Savior" far better than we ever can. One of the most enduring symbols of that ancient, persecuted church is the fish (ΙΧΘΥΣ in Greek) which is an acronym for J(I)esus Ch(X)rist, G(Θ)od's S(Υ)on, the S(Σ)avior. As you live your life, may God keep your focus on Jesus, your Savior and Deliverer, who has rescued you from darkness and brought you into his kingdom.

✠

Be What God Has Made You: More Than a Conqueror!

In all these things we are more than conquerors through him who loved us. (Romans 8:37)

"What do you want to be when you grow up?" As a teacher who helped out with post-graduation career planning for high school students, I asked that question literally hundreds of times. I've gotten lots of different answers, from the incredibly specific to the disturbingly vague. Most kids honestly have no idea (but they're pretty sure they want to go to college first). I shouldn't be too hard on them, though, since I'm not positive I've answered the question for myself yet.

However, one answer that I've never heard to that question is "king." We know that a person can't just choose to become a king; that role is usually passed on to certain people whether they want it or not. But if we were allowed to daydream a bit, wouldn't it be nice to be a king? The pay and benefits are great. Dynastic succession would make sure your kids were taken care of (one way or the other). All in all, being a king would be a great job — especially when it came to dealing with your enemies.

King Charles of the Franks, for example, vastly expanded his kingdom by a long period of war and conquest. He fought in innumerable battles, won most of them, and as Emperor Charlemagne united Europe under a kingdom that lasted for centuries. Centuries earlier, a Macedonian king named Alexander conquered most of the known world in one of the most successful military campaigns in history. His great empire helped set the Greek-speaking stage on which the drama of our salvation was unfolded.

Even though none of us have ever seriously considered becoming a king, it is still true that we are, in a sense, kings — not of an earthly political realm, but as followers of Jesus Christ we are heirs of his kingdom and beneficiaries of his mighty conquest of sin, death, and the devil. Paul confidently writes, "The Lord will rescue me from every evil attack and will bring me safely to his heavenly kingdom" (2 Timothy 4:18). Through his resurrection, Jesus "has destroyed all dominion, authority and power. For he must reign until he has put all his enemies under his feet. The last enemy to be destroyed is death" (1 Corinthians 15:24-26). This kingdom, this victory is ours. Peter promises that we "will receive a rich welcome into the eternal kingdom of our Lord and Savior Jesus Christ" (2 Peter 1:11).

Yes, amen. Jesus is our conquering, victorious king. His victory is our victory. But be careful getting too attached to that image of Christ as a conquering victorious King. There is a small catch. The first thing that Jesus conquers is *us*. Jesus' work on Calvary's cross conquered sin — the sin in our hearts. The enemies that he cuts down with his "sharp, double-edged sword" (Revelation 2:12) are sinners — sinners like you and me.

"See, the day of the LORD is coming — a cruel day, with wrath and fierce anger — to make the land desolate and destroy the sinners within it" (Isaiah 13:9). Jesus battles sin and fights sinners, and he wins every time. Imagine having all the glory, power, and righteous wrath of an Almighty King turned against *you*. That was our position as exiles from Christ's holy kingdom, and that is what we deserve each day for our many sins. There are times we need to be genuinely afraid of the Rider on the white horse, the one called Faithful and True (Revelation 19:11) — for we are neither faithful nor true.

Jesus' law brings us to our knees in repentance, so that we despair of our own strength and goodness and cry out to him for aid (Psalm 34; Jonah 3). Jesus wields his double-edged sword in our hearts, cutting away all that hinders us from growing closer to him (Matthew 5:30; Hebrews 12:1). Jesus gives us victory over sin and death by his own precious blood, which he poured out on the cross in the process of winning the greatest Victory of all (1 Corinthians 15:57; 1 John 1:7).

Because of Christ's sacrifice for sin, our sins are forgiven. By the work of the Faithful and True, we are made faithful and true. Because we belong to Christ, the Victorious Conqueror, we are victors and conquerors. Like a chess pawn that makes it to the last row on the chessboard and becomes a queen, those who are "faithful, even to the point of death" receive a "crown of life" (Revelation 2:10) — a share in God's eternal kingdom.

It is a foregone conclusion that we will face hardships in this life. Whether those are famine, nakedness, persecution, or the sword, or whether our own hardships are a bit more pedestrian, we have God's promise that we will not be separated from him. We are "more than conquerors" over all these things — but this is not to our credit, as though we were a Charlemagne or an Alexander the Great in our own right. We are not conquerors because of our own love and faith and devotion to the Lord. Our own efforts could never be enough to conqueror anything. No, we are conquerors "through him who loved us." In fact, through Jesus, we are "more than conquerors" — we are sharers, heirs, and beneficiaries of *his* divine conquest.

✠

Conclusion:

Be What God Has Made You!

Only let us live up to what we have already attained (Philippians 3:16).

Remember that old Saturday-morning cartoon image of a character faced with an important decision, with an angel perched on one shoulder and a devil on the other? The angel and the devil would each present their case as the character mulled over his choices, nodding in turn at the wisdom of his supernatural advisors. Usually, as I remember it, the angel ended up getting stabbed by a pitchfork and the character would follow the "bad" advice, with predictably humorous results.

As entertaining as that image is, it fundamentally misses the point of how we as Christians navigate our way through the myriad of ethical choices we make each day. We're not some morally-neutral third-party observer, carefully weighing God's advice against Satan's temptations, with the perfectly free will necessary to make the correct, unbiased decision each time. We're not above the fray, weighing our options from a safe distance. We're intensely part of the battle. We *are* the angel *and* the devil, both at the same time, fighting against ourselves in an internal, cosmic struggle.

St. Paul describes our frustrating, self-contradictory situation in Romans 7:14-24:

> We know that the law is spiritual; but I am unspiritual, sold as a slave to sin. I do not understand what I do. For what I want to do I do not do, but what I hate I do... I know that nothing good lives in me, that is, in my sinful nature. For I have the desire to do what is good, but I cannot carry it out. For what I do is not the good I want to do; no, the evil I do not want to do — this I keep on doing... So I find this law at work: When I want to do good, evil is right there with me. For in my inner being I delight in God's law; but I see another law at work in the members of my body, waging war against the law of my mind and making me a prisoner of the law of sin at work within my members. What a wretched man I am! ... I myself in my mind am a slave to God's law, but in the sinful nature [I am] a slave to the law of sin.

Or, again, as the theologians put it, we are *simul justus et peccator*: at the same time saint and sinner. This side of heaven, we will never be completely rid of the effects of the Fall; we will continue to struggle against the natural consequences of Adam's sin for our entire lives, even as we also deal with the individual fallout of our own sins and sinfulness. We do not have the perfectly free will to choose the good in every situation. Even though we want to do good, we are not always capable of it. And sometimes, even when we are capable of it, we just don't want to. "When I want to do good, evil is right there with me."

What is the solution to this "identity crisis"? It's not a little cartoon devil on our shoulder that we're fighting against — it's ourselves! How do we resolve this inner struggle? How can we live like this? What can we do? Paul asks the same question at the end of this section: "Who will rescue me from this body of death?" (Romans 7:24).

The answer, for Paul and for us, comes in the very next verse: "Thanks be to God — through our Lord Jesus Christ" (Romans 7:25). Through Jesus Christ, we have an identity that is firmly rooted and grounded in his promises, in his Word, and in his very Person. Yes, we are altogether corrupted by sin, constantly struggle against it, and daily sin much. Yes, we are sinners. Yet we are and will remain *forgiven* sinners by grace, through faith in Jesus Christ. Jesus exchanged places with us, took our sin even unto death on a cross, and gave us a new identity. Another theological truism simply yet profoundly describes our new selves: "We are by grace what Christ is by nature."

Throughout this book, we've been looking at that identity in detail. We've seen how our positional standing before God has been changed by our Spirit-wrought faith in Christ. We have looked at how our own self-perception is radically different because of our new identity. And we have seen our relationships changing, both with other believers and with the world at large. We have been encouraged, in the words of Philippians, to "live up to what we have already attained" — to be what God has made us.

Until Jesus returns to bring us to glory, the re-created new person who lives in us by faith will never fully triumph over our old, sinful nature. But by God's grace, each day can be a day when we "take off our old self" and "put on the new self, which is being renewed in knowledge in the image of its Creator" (Colossians 3:9-10).

God has not given us an angel that sits on our shoulder telling us what to do. He does not whisper advice into our ears, or beat the devil over the head with a cartoon halo. What God has done, however, is more amazing, more spectacular, and more powerful than any Saturday morning animated morality play. We are not just enabled to live righteously, as if all we needed was an extra spiritual boost. We're not just told to be righteous, as if we merely needed a fail-safe set of divine directions. No. We're not just called to be righteous — we *are* righteous. What God commands, he always does for us in and through Christ. In Jesus, *God has made you what he wants you to be.*

Now, Christian, go out and be what God has made you!

✠

Be What God Has Made You!

Be What God Has Made You!

Note

Proceeds from the sale of this book go to help translate the Word of God into languages that do not yet have a Bible. Visit http://www.LBT.org for more information.

To learn more about Chris Pluger's work of Bible translation in Zambia among the Nsenga people, visit http://theplugers.wordpress.com.

Please pray for those who do not yet have Bibles in languages that they can read and understand. In the meantime, read your English Bible!

Made in the USA
Middletown, DE
25 May 2022